Church and Religious Diversity

Reimagining Church as Event: Perspectives from the Margins
Series Editors: George Zachariah and Sudipta Singh

In these eleven volumes, a collective of Indian theologians envisions Church as an Event that happens in particular contexts in the life of the communities at the margins. They argue that in the life of the communities who experience on their bodies the violence and hegemony of dominant power relations, morality, and religious dogmas and practices, the church happens as countercultural experiences that disrupt the logic of the prevailing order. These experiences enable and empower them to affirm and celebrate their differences, knowledges and beauty even as they weave their liberation. Church as event is a call to rising to life, creating life-flourishing communities that live out the foretaste of the reign of God.

Titles in this Series

Church and Religious Diversity Joshua Samuel and Samuel Mall
Church and Gender Justice Aruna Gnanadason
Faith in the Age of Empire Y.T. Vinayaraj
Dalitekklesia: A Church from Below Raj Bharath Patta
Church and Climate Justice Vinod Wesley
Church and Disability Samuel George
Church and Diakonia in the Age of COVID-19 Mothy Varkey
Decolonising Oikoumene Gladson Jathanna
Church and Human Sexuality Arvind Theodore
With Many Voices: Liturgies in Context Viji Varghese Eapen (Ed.)
The Word becoming Flesh George Zachariah

Church and Religious Diversity

Joshua Samuel
and
Samuel Mall

2020

Church and Religious Diversity - jointly published by the Indian Society for Promoting Christian Knowledge (ISPCK), Post Box 1585, Kashmere Gate, Delhi-110006 and Council for World Mission, Singapore-338729.

ISBN: 978-93-88945-79-0

Kindle Edition: 978-93-88945-91-2

Cover Picture Credit : Immanuel Paul Vivekanandh K

Laser typeset by

ISPCK, Post Box 1585, 1654, Madarsa Road, Kashmere Gate, Delhi-110006 • *Tel:* 23866323

e-mail: ashish@ispck.org.in • ella@ispck.org.in
website: www.ispck.org.in

*This book was made possible through
the kind contribution of the Council for World Mission*

Contents

Foreword

Discernment and radical engagement (Dare) is an initiative of the Council for World Mission (CWM) to enable faith communities to *clarify what it means to engage in* public witness to God's justice and peace in a corrupt and conflicted world.

> The mission of Dare is conceived as the coming together of (a) the *radical soul* of discernment and sense-making in theology and biblical criticism; (b) the yearnings for *signifying engagement* that rise out of the slums of modernism and the valleys of despair; and (c) the commitment to redemption songs that *inspire disturbance* at the hubs of power.

As part of the DARE initiative, each region of CWM is invited to prepare and share biblical and theological resources on current themes and issues being considered by CWM, drawing upon the experiences and resources from the region.

Interfaith Engagement, Ecumenism and Inclusive communities against dehumanising social categorisations are the themes for the book series undertaken by the South Asia region of CWM. The thrust is centred on **Reimagining Church as Event: Perspectives from the Margins.** It calls to the fore persons living in the margins and highlights their voice, their narratives and their passion for a rearrangement of life in communities, as we know it, and a commitment to rise to life and to break out from Babylon. These books are intended for the use of lay people, pastors and evangelists as well as for theological students and seminaries. The series offer stories and narratives, analyses, liturgical resources, biblical, theological and ethical reflections, and missional/praxis proposals.

Church is an event that happens at the margins of contemporary life. Church happens as an epiphanic event where the divine presence is manifested and experienced in the pathos, struggles, contestations and harmonies of everyday existence. Church happens in those spaces where we celebrate the presence of Jesus, the Christ, in the flourishing of life. Church happens when we are transformed by one another, and inspired and enabled to engage in the transformative politics of the reign of God. Church happens whenever and wherever spirit-filled communities reclaim their subversive moral agency and contest the logic and practices of domination and exclusion. Church happens when the community experiences the healing power of the wounded healer and join Jesus in this risk-taking mission, despite the wounds we bear. To reimagine Church requires courage and commitment to engage in the mission of nurturing and organising communities of resistance and healing. This book series is a humble attempt at exposing and encouraging this radical expression of Church.

I appreciate and thank all those who are associated with this series, the authors, the contributors, the publishers and the editors. I commend this book series in the hope and prayers that they will help the faith communities in South Asia, and beyond, to *discern God's presence in community and dare to engage* in ways that re-present the God of life in communities and in the public square, *Rising to Life: Living out the New Heaven and New Earth.*

Colin Cowan
General Secretary
Council for World Mission

Introduction

*John J. Thatamanil**

Does it bear saying? Reality itself feels out of joint in this historical moment. A pandemic has turned the world upside down. Strangely, and I say this cautiously given the terrible toll taken by this disease, that is not the worst of it. Quite possibly no period in history has been better prepared to deal with such an outbreak. Precisely the networks of interconnection that make global transmission possible are also the very networks that might have led to a speedy resolution if nations joined together, shared knowledge, found solidarity in common purpose and arrested this death-dealing virus.

But just in this moment, another pandemic has afflicted billions on the planet: an international axis of xenophobia has been mobilised and diffused by poisoned tongued populists who deploy hate to consolidate their powers—hatred of the other whether that be the Muslim other or Dalits in India, Black Americans and Muslims in the United States, violence towards Indigenous persons and the land itself in Brazil, and misogyny and hatred of sexual minorities everywhere. Fear and hatred of the other continue to be powerful toxins, a lethal comorbidity factor in just those nations in which COVID-19 is exacting its heaviest toll. Majoritarian populism plus SARS-CoV-2 is deadly. Surprise, surprise, populist hate merchants, it turns out, have no interest in or capacity for responsible governance. Incompetence does not begin to describe the likes of Donald Trump, Narendra Modi and Jair Bolsonaro: not only do they make terrible leaders but they undermine the institutions in their care.

And, if that were not enough, the entire planet and our fellow creatures are in dire peril due to the looming climate catastrophe. We are living and dying through the sixth great extinction, and sober-minded scientists are predicting the end of human civilisation itself. Here, the chief death-dealing factor is an omnivorous death-dealing capitalism that pretends that infinite growth is possible on a final planet. A handful of extremely wealthy capitalists and their corporations are taking down the human species and countless other species in our wake.

In times such as this, is not interreligious dialogue a frivolous luxury, perhaps best left to idle academic elites? Should not dire issues such as these take precedence? What to the church is interreligious dialogue? After all the church itself seems unmoored and unsure of its place in the world. Should it not then devote itself to its own mission rather than take up the work of dialogue?

The answer to these questions, as Dr. Joshua Samuel and Rev. Samuel Mall make clear, must be an emphatic no. Perhaps there were once upon a time forms of dialogue conducted around dialogue tables in which privileged elites gathered to share in peaceable conversations that made no difference to the world's travails. But our authors make transparent that dialogue does not have to look like the private preoccupation of armchair philosophers and theologians. I myself wonder if interreligious dialogue among the pioneers was ever so placid and trivial. It is all too easy to caricature those first predecessors who vulnerably ventured into new terrain seeking understanding, solidarity and friendship. Are such things luxuries? Are not Christians who are commanded to love of neighbour by their Lord compelled by faith to cultivate such virtues and relationships?

In an era in which suspicion and hatred of the other seems the reigning and demonic spirit of the age, what could be more countercultural and more urgent than loving labour of interreligious dialogue? To spend time learning from and about our religious neighbours is a daring and healing gambit in an era marked by divisiveness. To recognise that your devotion to God by another name and by rituals other than mine need not hinder but might actually deepen not only my relationship with you but my relationship to God—that is the goal of the kind of deep, vulnerable and courageous interreligious dialogue imagined in this book.

Through dialogue, I come to learn that you *in your very difference* are a gift and treasure. Until I learn to love you and love to learn from you precisely because you are not me and do not think like me, I am not yet a servant of the lowly Galilean who commanded me to love neighbour and, yes, even enemy alike. If my goal is to erase you in your otherness, deprive you of your difference, and transform you into my own likeness, then how can I claim to love you? If my goal is to undo just those convictions and practices that give you life, then how can I claim to love you as you are? And, how can I claim to love the God whom I cannot see if I do not love my neighbours in their very difference?

Interreligious dialogue is an act of resistance. When I commit myself to such dialogue, I refuse to be manipulated by those who tutor me to hate the other—the other whose skin is darker, the other whose sexuality is different, the other who prays differently than I do. I affirm that life together across the divide of religious difference is more precious to me than feeling superior at your expense.

A Christianity that believes that it has no need for its religious neighbour, that presumes that God has not given witness to Godself outside of the church is not the God whose love Jesus the Christ enfleshed. Our authors wisely and prophetically ask us to imagine a church that learns from her religious neighbours just as Jesus himself learned from the Canaanite woman. How can we claim to follow a Jesus who learns from Jew and Gentile alike when we ourselves refuse to do as he did? How dare we presume that we have everything to give and nothing to receive and to learn?

None of this large-hearted openness to the other means that interreligious dialogue has to be reduced to handholding, although handholding, of course, is infinitely superior to fist-throwing. But interreligious dialogue can be more daring. It can strive to engage in common work on behalf of a just and sustainable world. Hindus, Christians and Muslims can join together to combat communalism and the forces of predatory capitalism. And, as trust between communities grows, we can even dare to talk about the damaging features of our own traditions always mindful though of Jesus' teaching that we dare not aim to remove the speck from our neighbour's eyes when a log remains in our own.

This book demonstrates that interreligious dialogue has arrived at new maturity. The deepest level of dialogue, whether between persons or between religious communities, is one in which honesty is possible and, when through that honesty, the difficult work of reconciliation and justice-making can take place. The authors rightly insist, "Dialogue is an ethical imperative." When we can tell the truth about each other and about ourselves, religious communities are empowered to join together to transform the world in the direction of God's reign. That is the kind of daring dialogue envisioned herein.

* **Dr. John J. Thatamanil** serves Union Theological Seminary, New York, USA, as Associate Professor of Theology and World Religions.

Chapter 1

Church as an Event
and Religious Diversity

Introduction

Religious experiences are the result of relationships between the divine, the human and the world, and any discussion on the church as an event has thus to be explored in terms of how it developed in history. What was the theological understanding that guided its establishment and how did this affect its relations with other religious traditions in South Asia? Culture and geographical context thus become significant to understand how Christianity emerged in the region.

Christian identities across the world have been informed by and formed in dialogue with other religious faiths. To think of Christianity (or any religious tradition for that matter) as a monolithic entity would be a gross mistake. In other words, the church has always been influenced by religious plurality. But this (obvious) historical truth (only) raises a number of questions: Is the church being 'affected' by other traditions good or bad? Should the church look at religious diversity as a problem to be addressed or as a demonstration of divine possibility/ies? How should the church relate to other faiths, the traditions themselves and their practitioners? In this chapter we will explore how the church emerged in Asian settings and on the changed context of South Asia.

Why Church as an Event?

The Business Dictionary defines 'event' as an "occurrence happening at a determinable time and place, with or without the participation of human agents. It may be part of a chain of human occurrences as an effect of a preceding occurrence and as a cause of succeeding occurrence." The word 'event' thus brings forth numerous considerations that are essential to understanding the identity of the church in relation to the historical contexts it emerged, the contexts in which it underwent change, and the context in which it exists today, even as opening possibilities of how it should/would be in the future. In other words, it brings forth a dialogical process of understanding of the past, the present and the future of the church and its relations to the community and other religions.

The church as an institution has undergone various changes since its inception. The Second Ecumenical Council of the Vatican (1962–65), or Vatican II, explains the changing nature of the church in the modern world. Vatican II brought about a significant change in how the church viewed itself in relation to the world. Before Vatican II, biblical principles were applied directly to the context at hand; thus theology became the first step to interpreting the context, and consequently the church became a hierarchically authoritative structure. Vatican II turned this approach on its head and brought forth an understanding where the church is first and foremost "people of God." A sense of shared authority between the church and the world became the criterion to understand its identity. Now the theological enterprise began with a careful analysis of the context before turning to the Bible for pastoral implication. Theological reflection became the second step. It is now a given that the analysis of social context is essential to describe and understand the church. This is the significance of using the word 'event' for the church. An event is never static, it is ever-changing; it is not rigid and it refers to a significant point in time when a task is completed.

The word 'event' also talks about relationships. In order to successfully conduct an event, its planning and organisation have to be meticulous. Needless to mention that 'event management' has become a booming business. The business aspect may be overlooked in this discussion, but the relationship aspect is significant for the church. The Greek word for the church, '*Ekklesia*,' defines this relationship efficiently; it means that the church is an organised body around Christ, with an elder appointed as head by the apostles. It is, therefore, not a club but a community. It shares a double relationship, one with Christ and the other with the world. This double relationship has become the criterion on which the church views and engages with society. We will explore the 'event' of the church in its historical setting and how the church expressed its relationship with society and religious diversity in its nascent stage in South Asia.

Church: The Event that Was

Christian mission in Asia was carried out in aggressive and invasive ways. As a result, mission was only seen through the lens of triumphalism. Christianity and its relationship with colonialism thus need to be relooked from the perspective of the margins.

Theological Background of Missionaries and Social Separation

Christian religion came to South Asia through European missionaries. These were from both the Roman Catholic and Protestant Churches influenced by the Pietistic movement. John Weborg describes the theological mindset of missionaries thus:

> Protestant missionaries, particularly Ziegenbalg, Plutschau and Schwarts received their training at university of Halle, the great centre of pietistic and evangelical Christianity. These men were taught by the well known and pious professor Francke and his son. Theologically, the main concept in which Prof. Francke, like his predecessor Spencer believed, was the concept of second or new birth. He himself had a dramatic conversion experience in 1686. The basis of Halle theology was infallibility of the scriptures. In this expression, a special emphasis was laid on personal holiness and the concern for another world. Prof. Francke's theology of new birth included five main points: realisation of men's invalidity and sinfulness; recognition of divine illumination of human will to do the truth; experience God's act of conversion which includes the struggle against the old nature; assurance of salvation means becoming aware of God's working in one's life; and living a life of newly recreated person which includes a new style of life. (Weborg 1886: 202, Quoted in Massey 2014:79)

In addition to this theological background, James Massey observes that missionaries from the Pietistic movement involved themselves in social work, which was considered secular and secondary to missionary or spiritual obligation (Massey 2014: 80). Pietism influenced Germany and other parts of Europe, England and America.

The Presbyterian mission to India represented a similar theological outlook. John Webster says the reigning theology of the Presbyterian Church in the nineteenth century was Princeton theology (Webster 1976: 31). Their message can be summed up in the following manner,

- All men are sinners and will therefore be punished by God who is Holy and righteous.

- People by themselves cannot satisfy God's demand for holiness and righteousness

- God in His love sent His Son to suffer and die, thus taking upon Himself the atonement for men's sin

- Men are saved from their sins only by believing in what God in Christ has done for them

- This salvation is offered to everyone freely and should be accepted with repentance, faith, thanksgiving and holiness of life (Webster 1976: 83).

In short, missionary message was a combination of the Pauline theology of justification by faith in Christ alone and the substitutionary theology of atonement. This theological outlook characterised missionaries' communication with local people and religion. The sacred and the secular were considered separate and distinct and the Christian worldview was clearly other-worldly. It was extremely triumphalistic, individualistic, focusing on personal piety, and, by normative standards, above other scriptures. Consequently, Christianity became exclusivist, marginalising other religions and religious scripture, considering itself to be true and others false. This missionary theology drove a wedge between Christianity and local religions. Gnana Robinson, an Old Testament Bible scholar who was born into a Christian family in Tamil Nadu, India, describes this separation as social apartheid. Citing his own experience, he points out that as children he and his friends were never allowed in any social function of other religions because of the fear of contamination by participating in Hindu rituals and eating the food placed before idols (Robinson 2000: 84).

This is also true of an experience that this writer had with the pastors of a diocese in the Church of North India. I was once invited as a resource person for a pastors' conference in Amritsar in Punjab. As part of exposure to local culture, we were taken to the Golden Temple, the Sikhs' most important pilgrimage site, in Amritsar. When I took *prasad* (a devotional offering made to a god, typically consisting of food that is later shared among devotees) from the temple and offered it to the pastors to eat, they saying they did not eat food offered to other gods as it would pollute them. This idea of purity and pollution is still a part of the theological outlook of people and it creates a sense of divide between religions Such theology only fosters exclusion.

Sense of Superiority: Structural Separation

South Asia was and is culturally, linguistically and religiously plural. In that context one factor that strained the relationship between Christianity and other religions was a sense of superiority attached with Christian missionaries and Christian religion. Bishop Lesslie Newbigin of the Church of South India points out that from the beginning of missionaries' arrival in India, they were considered as 'Sahibs' (lords) (Newbigin 1984: 1). This sense of racial superiority not only strained relationships between Christians and people of other religious persuasions but also between new converts and missionaries. This sense of superiority made missionaries feel they did not need to identify with the majority of the population.

Golaknath, who became an outstanding leader of the Christian community in Punjab, India, was baptised in 1837 and was ordained in 1857. His assertions would explain to us the sense of superiority with which missionaries practised. During the Punjab Missionary Conference in 1858-59, he pointed out,

Missionary was in a social position and had cultural attainments so far superior to those of native Christians and that the latter could not be expected to excite much fellow feeling from the former. Converts, in turn, tended to look upon the missionaries not only as 'paid agents of religious company' but also as patron who is to look after their wellbeing as well as their moral and spiritual development. He therefore recommended that the missionaries treat converts as friends and mix with them as much as possible, that they never get angry with converts but treat them with due deliberation and impartiality. (quoted in Webster 2007: 124)

This observation from a convert is significant. The general public saw the missionary as superior and the missionaries treated themselves as superior to the local people. John Webster Grant points out that missionaries had a sense of racial superiority (Grant 1961: 5). Consequently, this sense of superiority not only damaged relationships between missionaries and converts, but also between Christianity and other religions. The church thus developed an identity characterised by separation and not communion.

Initial Mission Strategy of Missionaries: Separation from Within

Missionary involvement in Indian society shows that missionaries focused on converting people who were from dominant sections of society. As missionaries were educated and depended on reasoning and intellectual argument to convince others of their Christian religious conviction, they settled in cities and made initial contacts with educated people and those in dominant positions. They tried to penetrate society from the top. Hence, they were only concerned with preaching the gospel to the affluent in society or the urban people. This approach did not bear much fruit as conversions were few and far between. Since most of the converts were from among the upper castes, Webster observes, by the end of the nineteenth century, Christian converts had developed their own aristocracy (Webster 1976: 78-79). Massey observes that this attitude and theology of missionaries that focused on superiority was influenced by their own context in European society which was marred by divisions between feudal lords and commoners (Massey 2014: 73-83).

However, irrespective of missionaries' approach that focused on the dominant sections of society, people belonging to the lower castes and other marginalised communities got converted to Christianity in thousands all over India. These conversion movements are defined as "Mass Movements." These were grassroots movements carried out with local support and initiative. When missionaries saw this trend, they confined themselves to the role of administering baptism and the Lord's Supper. This conversion trend puzzled the missionaries and it was clear that they were not pleased with this development. In fact, they saw people from the lower castes converting to Christianity as an embarrassment. A letter written by J.C.R. Ewing to the Board of Foreign Missions on 19 March 1884 described the trend of conversions from among the lower castes as "raking rubbish into the church" (cited by Webster 1976: 60).

Massey divides missionaries into two groups: one, those who were concerned about increasing conversions from among the lower castes for sheer numbers; and two, those who were opposed to the idea of accepting converts from the lower castes (Massey 2014, 85). The missionaries came from a context where discrimination on the basis of class was prevalent; now they embraced discrimination on the basis of caste in Indian society. The expression of this discrimination was symbolised in how the Lord's Supper was administered. There were separate cups for people belonging to the upper and lower castes. If there was only one cup, the upper caste people would take the communion first.

There were numerous other separations too, between the culture of Christianity and the culture of Hinduism, between Christianity and Hinduism as religions, and between the oppressed and the dominant. This separation was social as well as cultural. This separation would later define how different theologians tried to address Christianity and its relationship to local religions after the collapse of the British Empire. This attitude resulted in an exclusive theology of religions.

Church and Theology of Religions

There is no doubt that the missionaries left a lasting effect on local religions. However, since the majority of conversions were from among the oppressed community, theology did not pick up local cultural elements. Christianity was seen in opposition to native religions. Developing in tandem with colonialism, Christianity was considered to be a superior religion. As Eric J. Sharpe, scholar in the history of modern Christian mission and interreligious dialogue, says, the majority of evangelical missionaries at work in India in the 1850s and beyond tended to regard Hinduism in its least favourable aspect and to contrast it in their own mind with Christianity at its best (Sharpe 1965: 28). The annual reports of missionary societies in America, the memoirs and books written by missionaries on India, and their published sermons provide insights on how Hindu religion and culture was seen as spiritual misery in a benighted land (Pathak 1967: 78). The missionaries fostered an image of backwardness about India in their own countries. They certainly desired the best for Indians, but their method of achieving this through the unguided criticism of religion and culture was misguided. Therefore, a sense of power was attached to the Christian missionary as a person, Christian mission as a strategy, and Christianity as a religion. People were looked down as objects of mission, and other religions were seen as evil. However, there were positive interactions by missionaries like William Carey and works of education all over India, but by and large a strained relationship was the norm. It is evident that in colonial understanding, religions had clear demarcated boundaries and belonging to a religion was conceived in exclusive terms. Thus, the understanding of religion was developed neglecting cultural, social, economic and political aspects of life and its relation to religion. In addition, Christianity was seen as one among many religions but with a privileged position. Religious diversity was thus seen as a problem and threat.

Developing from such an understanding of religion, missionary theologies led to the development of personalised dimensions of spirituality, which further strained interreligious relationships. Theology was primarily Christology, and the approach to atonement did not probe the question of why the death of Christ was necessary to make visible the redemptive love of God. It only probed the questions of the purpose of Christ coming into the world and its relation with humanity. Atonement only questioned incarnation (Baillie 1956: 158). Therefore, the atoning work of Jesus on the cross was not directed towards tracing the ideal humanity to which we are called, but towards an extreme price which was paid for our salvation—in many cases *my* salvation (Ford & Higton 2009: 262). Therefore, personal experience and identification with Christ became the priority. Personal holiness was preferred over the corporate. Jesus was seen in individualistic terms. He was thus crucified for/by *me* for *my* salvation. The community perceived itself as one of sinners and believed there was no other redeeming reality besides Christ. Along with theology, the structure of the church aided the development of its exclusive character.

When the church came to India the threefold ministry of the Bishop, the Presbyter and the Deacon was maintained. As a result, a highly organised church emerged. It was highly sophisticated, democratic and set up with many legal safeguards. R.H.S. Boyd points out that, when such a church organisation was transplanted in India, it appeared very foreign, legalistic and unspiritual (Boyd 1974: 68). Church union movements like the Church of South India and the Church of North India tried to correct this error by envisioning a church that was self-propagating, self-governing and self-sustaining. It tried to get rid of its colonial clothing. Because of its approach towards local culture, religion and mission strategies that were discriminatory, the church was unable to gather sufficient converts. However, a social revolution was building up, and the history of the church was about to change. Marginalised communities were turning to Christ through local initiative and effort.

Conversion and Community: Appropriation of Christian Faith by the Marginalised

Marginalised communities perceived the event of the church differently. Conversion became a form of protest for them. Contrary to missionary theology and strategy, the marginalised in large numbers accepted Christianity. From the perspective of the margins, a few questions become significant to study such conversion events. What were the motives behind the conversions? What were the aspirations of the people in doing so? Did conversion change social location? What were the immediate and long-term effects of conversion? Was conversion limited to just a change of religion? Was it an effective strategy?

In mission work, Christian conversion can happen at two levels: at the individual level and the group level. In the Indian context, as J.W. Gladstone observes, the term 'group', 'people', or 'mass', theologically, refer to the common, despised people who are always oppressed and poor (Gladstone 1984: 96). Hence, the Christian mass conversion movements were genuinely the movements of the poor and the oppressed.

Conversion endowed the oppressed communities with a new identity. Conversion generally arises out of an internal conflict between the ideal and the actual self, is accompanied by guilt and a feeling of unattained possibilities, often involves pathological behaviour, and reveals natural self-healing tendencies of the personalities (Raj 2001: 25). It completes the journey from an unrecognised selfhood to a dynamic selfhood. This dynamic selfhood provides courage and self-respect and heals the communities of poor selfhood. At the same time, it projects the possibility of respect and recognition from others too. The future of the converts was dependent upon their actions and interests; it was not what anyone in the dominant community decided for them. Conversion by the marginalised communities was thus a protest against the dominant communities. This element of protest is properly summed up in the words of Lewis R. Rambo,

> Conversion takes place in a dynamic context. This context encompasses a past panorama of conflicting, confluent, and dialectical factors that both facilitate and express the process of conversion. Conversion is a process influenced not only by objective external forces but also by subjective, internal motivations, experiences and aspirations (Rambo 1993: 20).

Philip Peacock and Sathianathan Clarke make three observations at work in Dalit conversion. First, it is an encounter of God-in-Christ that is loving, forgiving and freeing each person and the whole community. In encounter with Christ, God becomes a closer reality, well within reach. The second involves the rejection and reformation of symbols of God, human beings and the world inherited from caste-based Hinduism. These considerations become important because they address what sort of humanity is legitimised by God. The third is the element of hope. Salvation and humanisation are seen as result of human activity that teaches one how to live and work towards its realisation (Peacock and Clarke 2010: 192-194). These three observations do not provide a mandate to convert but sets forth the gifts that conversion will bring when the one who is converting decides to convert without external pressure. These three considerations become valid only and if the processes of conversion are approached by the one who wishes to convert.

The missionary call to convert was located in an approach that centred on the rejection of a previous religion and not transformation. It overlooked the socio-political and religio-cultural realities of oppression and injustice. Rejection would have resulted in lost memory of past happenings; hope for change would have become other-worldly. Therefore, change in religion was a social protest by the marginalised communities. These were aimed at gaining equality.

Religion provides the marginalised with contextually relevant interpretation of social reality. Social vision and emancipatory identity are significant in the moral formation of the marginalised and the society at large. These social visions motivated the marginalised to convert, not missionary theology. Religion was seen as transformative, and conversion was an agency that aided such transformation.

Co-opting the Marginalised: Inculturation

Conversion for the marginalised was a 'way out.' Getting out of a discriminatory religion was the priority. Samuel Jayakumar describes this as "progressive conversion experience" (Jayakumar 1999:5). Christianity came for the oppressed as an agency. The immediate consequences of conversion were good; it gave the oppressed a sense of acknowledged selfhood which was not discriminatory. It gave them confidence, strength, new life, new identity, and dignity amidst oppression. It created hope for the poor and the oppressed. Through conversion, the marginalised were released from centuries of misery and oppression.

Conversions brought about social awareness and transformation. Along with the character of revolt, conversion had a healing effect on the oppressed communities. But these liberative aspects (social) of conversion were overlooked as the marginalised were still away from formal theological programme. Separation was only seen in terms of culture through the medium of religion. Inevitably, the dominant culture became the norm through which cultural and religious separation was addressed. Overcoming this cultural separation defined the Christian attitude towards religious diversity.

As a result, the Indian theological system, as it developed, was obsessed by the Brahminic (dominant) tradition in Hinduism. A.P. Nirmal points out that the Indian theological system until the 1980s had been dominated by a culture that represented the elite of society. It was the work of the elites expressing the worldview of the elites. Mapping the theological tradition until the 1980s, Nirmal makes the following observation,

> To speak in terms of the traditional Indian categories, Indian Christian Theology, following the Brahminic tradition, has trodden the *jnana marga*, the *bhakti marga* and the *karma marga*.

In Brahmabandhav Upaddhyaya, we have a brilliant theologian who attempted a synthesis of Sankara's advaita vedanta and Christian theology. In Bishop A. J. Appasamy, we had a *bhakti margi* theologian who tried to synthesize Ramanuja's Vishista Advaita with Christian theology. In M. M. Thomas we have a theologian who has contributed to theological anthropology at the international level and who laid the foundation for a more active theological involvement in India - the karma marga. In Chenchiah, we find an attempt to synthesize Christian theology with Sri Aurobindo's Integral Yoga (Nirmal: 54-55).

It is therefore evident that the Indian Christian theological tradition neglected the socio-economic dimension of religion and society. Even the Indian ecumenical involvement and its allegiance to dialogue with other faiths have further extended the Brahminic ideology in theology. Nirmal calls this an obsession with the Brahminic tradition (Nirmal: 56). Efforts were made to reconcile Hinduism with Christianity. Such approaches overlooked the historical dimension of human life. Questions about religion and its relationship with other religions were limited to culture, language and symbols contained within that religion and not human life in its totality. The church and the theology of religion only focused on the aspect of inculturation as a means to address religious diversity. As a result, it co-opted mass movements as cultural movements aimed at conversion. The "problem" of relationship with other faiths became more important than the "problem" of the suffering community. The dominant culture became the norm in theology so much so that the needs and aspirations of the oppressed were forgotten and neglected.

Was such Exclusion Justified? Overcoming Separation

Baptism and conversion in a religious sense are related to each other, as without baptism the religious conversion process is considered to be incomplete. Those whose minds are conditioned by baptism as a rite see it as a form of separation. Being baptised and converted brings forth the idea of separation. For the oppressed communities, baptism meant a sort of separation. Separation from the older unrecognised, disrespected self. Even today, if someone converts, he/she is seen as separating oneself from the older self and from previous religion he/she followed. Is this whole idea of separation attached to baptism biblical? Is baptism a sort of separation? It was only after the act of baptism that the oppressed were considered, if not fully but partially, separate from their community who had not converted.

Christopher Duraisingh explicates that Christian baptism arose out of a particular cultural and religious context. It is a culturally conditioned rite and it arises neither from any specific imperative nor institution from our Lord Jesus (Duraisingh 1972: 9). In order to understand baptism, he also points out that the emphasis in recent New Testament studies is on the baptism of Jesus himself. He points out that Jesus's baptism included a total commitment for all his life, leading to the cross, death, resurrection and ascension, and therefore can the church confine the meaning of baptism to an initiation rite that seeks to bring numbers? (Duraisingh 1972:13) Therefore, contemporary understanding should highlight baptism, a) as means of individual grace, b) as a sacrament in the sense of inner transformation, c) as incorporation into the church, and d) as a re-enactment and re-presentation of God's redemptive work in Christ (Duraisingh 1972: 16 & Aleaz 1998: 345). The dominant motifs of baptism lead us to the correction of the distorted meaning of it.

Thus, baptism provides one with a new and radical form of identity which works for peaceful life together, breaking barriers of organised structures, secular or ecclesiastical. Thus, the traditional image of baptism as a separation from the original religious community needs to be corrected (Aleaz 1998: 346). Separation is only from sin and not from one's community. J. R. Chandran perfectly sums it up,

> Baptism rightly understood is, therefore, the sacrament of inclusive identification with the humanity with which Jesus identified with himself. It is a sacrament through which human beings transcend the human judgment of good and evil and overcome all temptation to exclusiveness. It is a sacrament of commitment to belong to the whole humanity which Christ has willed to redeem. It is the sacrament of commitment to work out all the implications of the love which God had revealed in Jesus Christ. Therefore, no exclusiveness and divisiveness can be associated with Christian baptism. If there is any justification for the concept of 'separation' associated with baptism, it can only be separation from exclusiveness and divisiveness which characterizes human beings in this fallen state (Chandran 1972: 56-58).

Through conversion, the marginalised tried overcoming the older unrecognised, discriminatory, exclusive and oppressive world. Conversion aimed at the creation of a just society, where love, respect and care of all was to become a lived reality. It was a protest against the idea of superiority based on purity and pollution. It also contributed in building up a better human existence/community characterised by mutual cooperation. This separation from the older self, however, was only seen in terms of separation from religion. Thereby, even after conversion discrimination continued within the church and outside of it.

Changing Theology of Church: Church as an Event in the Present

When theologians write as members of a society, community or a group, located in a particular boundary, be it political or social, theologies turn out to be contextual. Thus, theology takes into account the dynamics of society, its past, present and future. The past, present and future are three interrelated dynamics of any theological discourse. Varied and diverse contexts, varied and diverse theologies. Various factors have influenced modern theology. As David Ford puts it,

> Between the European middle ages and the end of nineteenth century there were many major events and transformation of life and thought, often originating in Europe but with global consequences. Chief among these have been Renaissance and Reformation, the colonization of the Americas, the enlightenment, The American and French Revolution, the rise of nationalism, the Industrial revolution and the development of natural sciences, technologies, medical sciences and human sciences. There has also been combined impact of bureaucracies, constitutional democracy, new means of warfare and of communication, mass media and public health programs and new movements in the art and philosophy and religion (Ford 1997: 1).

Modern theologies developed in response to these varied and complex developments. Theologies rejected, reformed or even reversed the implications of these developments. There were varied approaches and, as a result, some repeated past theology, some reformed it, while others transformed it. New approaches came to the forefront and the reality of God in relation to human beings and the world was revisited.

Missionary theology was challenged by a few events in history. The first was the two World Wars. They were instrumental in bringing about a change in the theology of the church. After the war people were deeply troubled by the pre-war Christian concept of God (Johnson 1987: 18). Weapons of mass destruction were at the disposal of human beings. Widespread death, suffering and destruction challenged the idea of God as great and infinite. Theology appeared to be too small in the context of widespread destruction of life in the post-war era. Identification of God with moral goodness was questioned as also the role of human beings in building an ideal society. Hope of overcoming suffering was lost and people suffered and died.

The wars also brought an end to the colonial empire; a new sense of nationalism developed in many countries as they gained independence from colonial rule. Such was the context of South Asia. In the case of India, theologians disrupted colonial theology by interpreting the Christian faith through Hindu scriptures. Thus, attempts were made to adapt Christianity in its colonial context.

Another factor that impacted theological methodology was the advent of Latin American liberation theology. Liberation theology that emerged in Latin America during the 1960s and 1970s recognised that the church had often sided with the oppressive structures of society and thereby declared that from now on it would stand on the side of the poor. This was a theology that was oriented towards the poor and the oppressed; they became the sources of theological discourse. It was an action-oriented theology as it recognised that theology should not be detached from social involvement and political action (McGrath 2001: 115-116). Liberation theology inspired the emergence of "Third world theology." Through liberation theology, the importance of social involvement and political action was highlighted; it stressed the need to discover the linkage of social, political, cultural and economic life settings of people. Experiences of suffering, deprivation, oppression and subjugation became sources of theologising. Theology developed from human situation and not scriptures; it became praxis-oriented. This change in methodology also influenced the Christian attitude towards other religions.

Challenges in the South Asian Context: The Future Event

With the fall of the colonial empire and formation of new nation states, the context of South Asia underwent a drastic transformation. Partition of nations led to widespread and uncontrolled violence. Since these partitions were religiously motivated, relationship between religions became strained. Partition of India is a perfect example of this religious animosity. People murdered each other in the name of religion. Thus, seeds for animosity between religions and between countries were sown.

South Asia is religiously, linguistically and culturally plural. Almost all the religions of the world are practised here. In such a plural world, dangers of religious extremism and fundamentalism are high.

Religious tensions are prevalent in every country of South Asia. Paul Knitter writes,

> Still today the battle cries of Protestants and Catholics in Northern Ireland, Buddhist and Hindus in Sri Lanka, of Sikhs and Hindus and Muslims in India are sad testimonies that religions continue to be more effective at motivating war than peace (Knitter 1992: 284, quoted in Robertson 2006: 18)

It is to be noted here that it is not religions but the rather naïve, literal, superficial interpretation of scripture that gives rise to fundamentalism. A few fundamentals of religion are projected to be representative of an entire religious tradition and this is further politicised by people in power. Through fundamentalism, the powerful gain control of all spheres of life whereas for others space is limited. It threatens equality and freedom and focuses on exercising control over others. This majoritarian control was evident when a million Tamils who toiled in the plantations of Sri Lanka were reduced to a stateless community so that they do not become a threat to majoritarianism in future (Selvaraj 2002: 66). However, this problem was corrected 40 years later.

South Asian countries are full of fundamentalist groups that try to exercise control over other people and religions. Religion and politics are confused in a South Asian setting so much so that politicisation of religion and cultural nationalism become means to garner votes. Fundamentalism, communalism and extremism become political strategies that divide people. It resists the practice of pluralism and openness, which is essential for peaceful religious coexistence.

Along with plurality, poverty defines the South Asian context; it is a land of glaring economic inequality and disparity. It is estimated that South Asia, which accounts for 22 per cent of the world population, houses 60 per cent of the world's poor. The report of human development in South Asia paints a gloomy picture of poverty and inequality in the region. The report states,

> South Asia is one of the fastest growing regions of the world in terms of economic growth. However, the benefits of current development strategies have so far not benefitted the majority of the population. There is an increase in poverty and inequality, especially in urban and peri-urban areas. Inadequate employment generation and persistence of low productivity employment in most sectors of the economy have resulted in an increase in deprivation (HDSA 2014: 47-48).

The gap between the rich and the poor is becoming wider. Among South Asian countries, India has the highest number of hungry people in the world. The statistics on wealth sharing is also dismal; Oxfam reports that 1 per cent of India's population takes home 73 per cent of the country's wealth. The situation in other countries is no different.. Asia's wealth gap is the highest in the world. Poverty and inequality are inescapable realities of South Asia. Free-market economy has benefited only the rich. It was believed that the fruits of liberalised economy and open market would trickle down to the poor, but it has only increased the wealth of the rich. Poverty is an inescapable reality in South Asia.

Rapid industrialisation and urbanisation in South Asia has resulted in extreme environmental degradation too. The air quality index in major South Asian cities is dismal, affecting the health of children and the aged the most. Air pollution has surpassed toxic levels. This makes cities more vulnerable to the adverse effects of climate change. The recent instances of floods in India, Bangladesh and Pakistan, and the earthquake in Nepal, are examples of how South Asian cities are among the most vulnerable in the world. The poor and slum-dwellers are the most vulnerable to natural disasters.

Lack of safe drinking water and pollution of waterbodies further affect the health of people. There has been a complete breakdown of interrelatedness of human life and ecology. Sustainable growth has given way to profit-oriented growth. Stress on farmers is increasing. The interdependence of humans and nature is overlooked for profit. The nations of South Asia have realised that climate change is real and have made efforts to reduce pollution and fall back on renewable energy to mitigate the damage already done. Continued commitment towards sustainable development can reduce the risk of climate change.

The position of women and girls is also dismal. In the patriarchal nature of South Asian societies, women lag behind in equality and equal opportunity. The 2016 report of Human Development in South Asia points out that,

> Women face adversity due to their low status in society, which
> has attributed to legal discrimination and violence. Over last
> one decade and a half, all the countries of South Asia have
> formulated a number of laws to empower women economically.
> However, the laws face a problem of ineffective implementation.
> As a result the region faces a high prevalence of violence against
> women in the form of honour killing, trafficking, feticide and
> so on (HDSA 2016: 21).

Compared with the annual report of 2002, the status of women
have made significant progress, but the fact is that the overall
picture remains grim. The report highlights that despite efforts
by the governments of South Asian countries in adopting policies
and laws that focus on women's empowerment, the culture
of patriarchy resists the progress of women. These issues will
become significant on how the church develops its theology
of religions. Church as an event in the present depends on
how issues pertaining to human life in all its complexities are
addressed.

Conclusion

We saw in this chapter how the church emerged in the South
Asian context. With their sense of superiority and pietistic
theological outlook, missionaries gave an exclusive charter to
the church. The critique of local culture was based on such a
sense of superiority. However, despite missionary theology, the
marginalised sections converted to Christianity in an attempt to
overcome their discrimination in society. Option for Christianity
was an option for liberation. However, the liberative elements in
conversion were gradually overlooked and the dominant ideology
became the norm through which conversions were reduced to
mere cultural separation. As colonial culture influenced mission
strategy, discrimination continued unabated.

The mid-twentieth century brought changes to theological methodology, and theologians and the church engaged themselves into re-evaluating Christian attitudes towards other religions. The present context offers many more challenges in multicultural and multireligious South Asian societies. The following chapters will focus on religious diversity in the present context of South Asia.

Bibliography

Nirmal, A.P. "Towards A Christian Dalit Theology" in *A Reader in Dalit Theology,* edited by A.P. Nirmal (Madras: GURUKUL, NA), 54-55.

Aleaz, K. P. *Theology of Religions: Birmingham Papers and Other Essays.* Calcutta: Moumita Publishers & Distributors: 1998.

Baillie, D.M. *God was In Christ.* London: Faber & Faber Limited, 1956.

Boyd, Robin H. S. *India and the Latin Captivity of the Church: The Cultural Context of the Gospel.* Great Britain: Cambridge University Press, 1974.

Chandran, J. R. "Baptism: A Scandal or a Challenge." *Religion and Society Vol XIX* No.1 (1972): 51 -58.

Christopher Duraisingh, "Some Dominant Motifs in The New Testament Doctrine of Baptism," in *Religion and Society Vol XIX* No.1 (1972), 5-17.

Clarke, Sathianathan & Philip Vinod Peacock. "Dalit and Religious Conversion: Slippery Identities and Shrewd Identifications." In *Dalit Theology in the 21st Century: Discordant Voices and Diverse Pathways.* Edited by Sathianathan Clarke, Deenbandhu Manchala and Philip Vinod Peacock. New Delhi: Oxford University Press.

Ford, David & Mike Higton, ed. *Jesus.*UK: Oxford University Press, 2009.

Ford, David F. "Introduction to Modern Christian Theology" in *The Modern Theologians,* Edited by David F. Ford Massachusetts: Blackwell Publishers, 1997.

Gladstone, J W. *Protestant Christianity and Peoples Movement in Kerala.* Trivandrum: Seminary Publications, 1984.

Grant, John Webster. *God's People in India.* Mysore: Christian Literature Society, 1961.

Human Development in South Asia 2014: Urbanization: Challenge and Opportunities, Mahbub ul Haq Human Development Centre, Karachi: CrossMedia. 2014

Human Development in South Asia 2016: Empowering Women in South Asia, Mahbub ul Haq Human Development Centre, Karachi: CrossMedia. 2016

Jayakumar, Samuel. *Dalit Consciousness and Christian Conversion: Historical Resources for Contemporary Debate.* Chennai: Mission Educational Books, 1999.

Johnson, Roger ed., *Rudolf Bultmann: Interpreting Faith in Modern Era.* London: Collin Liturgical Publications, 1987.

Knitter, Paul F. "Inter-religious Dialogue and the Unity of Humanity" in *Journal of Dharma,* Vol. XVI, NO. 4 (October- December 1992). 284

Newbegin, Leslie. *The Other Side of 1984.* Geneva: WCC 1984.

Massey, James. *Dalit Theology: History, Context, Text and Whole Salvation.* New Delhi: Manohar Pub., 2014.

McGrath, Alister E. *An Introduction to Christian Theology: 3rd Ed.* USA: Blackwell Publishers, 2001.

Muthiah, Selvaraj, "Reconciliation Among Political Victims" In *Inter-Cultural Asian Theological Methodologies: As Exploration.* Edited by Samson Prabhakar. Bangalore: SATHRI, 2002.

Nirmal, A.P. "Doing Theology From Dalit Perspective." In *A Reader In Dalit Theology.* Edited by A.P. Nirmal. Madras: GURUKUL, NA.

Pathak, Sushil Madhava. *American Missionaries and Hinduism: A Study of Their Contacts From 1813-1910.* New Delhi: Oriental Publishers, 1967

Raj, Y. Anthony *Social Impact of Conversion.* Delhi: ISPCK, 2001.

Rambo, Lewis R. *Understanding Religious Conversions.* New Heaven: Yale University Press, 1993.

Robertson, S. "Religion as Life Sustaining: A pluralist Perspective," *Religion and Society* Vol 51 No. 1 (March 2006): 1-20.

Robinson, Gnana, "From Apartheid to Dialogical Living: The need of the hour" In *Religion and Society Vol 46* No. 1& 2 (March- June 1999): 82-96

Sharpe, Erick J. *Not to Destroy but To Fulfill.* Sweden: Almqvist & Wiksells Boktryckeri AB, 1965.

Weborg, John. "Pietisma: The Fire Of God Which… Flames In The Heart Of Germany," in *Protestant Spiritual Tradition,* edited by Franck C. Sean, New York: Paulist Press, 1886.

Webster, John C. B. *The Christian Community and Change In The Nineteenth Century North India.* Meerut: Macmillan Company of India Ltd, 1976.

__________. *A Social History Of Christianity: North West India Since 1800.* New Delhi: Oxford University Press, 2007.

Chapter 2

Christian Engagement with Other Religious Traditions

Having reflected on the theme of religious diversity with the objective of reimagining the church as an event, in this chapter we move on to the practical manifestations of Christian interreligious engagement. When we speak of the church and religious diversity, one of the fundamental tasks for us is to ask how the church has related itself so far to other religious traditions. This question, I believe, will naturally lead us to the study and analysis of various forms and modes of Christian interreligious engagement which are represented under the broad category of interreligious dialogue (also referred to as interfaith dialogue, or just dialogue, in this book), which also includes interreligious practices and interreligious activism. However, while we acknowledge these conscious and intentional exchanges, we know that mutual engagement between religions happens, and in fact flourishes, through grass-roots level interaction between (different) faith communities. And what we often witness in these community-centred interreligious exchanges is the blurring of religious boundaries and the demonstration of the possibility of hybrid and multireligious identities. In other words, in religiously pluralistic contexts like South Asia (which, by the way, is true for most of the world today), multiple religious belonging among the 'ordinary' people reminds us that interreligious dialogue is not just a conversation between and among religious scholars or religious leaders, but rather a way of life.

Keeping in mind these different dimensions of Christian interreligious engagement, we begin this chapter with an overview of interreligious dialogue, focusing on its theological premise. Following this, we shall consider in brief the different types of dialogue. Thirdly, we will look at some of the problematic issues in dialogue. We will finally turn to the practice of multiple religious belonging which, though a new 'trend' in the West, is in fact a common reality in religiously pluralist contexts like South Asia.

Interreligious Dialogue

Even if since the first century of the Common Era the church has been in the midst of flourishing religious diversity—we shall return to this point again later in the book—it is in the nineteenth and twentieth centuries that it became a deliberate ecclesial motif. The nineteenth century witnessed the consolidation of the European colonial 'empires' across the world, particularly the establishment of the British Empire in South Asia, and the conspicuous presence of Christian missionaries in Asia and Africa, thanks to the spirit of eighteenth-century evangelicalism. In this context, as one might expect, there was naturally an increased movement and interaction between European Christians and people of other faiths in South Asia. However, much of this exchange that happened under the firm hand and the watchful eyes of the colonisers—the British in this case—

was not genuine or enthusiastic. Of course, there were quite a few exceptions, especially among South Asian Christians who were creative and adventurous. But for the most part, at least on an institutional level, the church was not eager to engage in interreligious conversations.

It is in the twentieth century that we see a more visible and bold engagement between Christianity and other religious traditions. This change in interreligious attitudes can be linked to a few noticeable reasons. By the 1930s and 1940s, more and more Asian and African countries gained independence from the chains of colonialism. Moreover, the Holocaust (and the two World Wars) revealed the unimaginable depths of evil that humans were capable of—although these were by no means singular if we recall the evils of slavery and colonialism among many others—and thereby the urgent need for humanity to strive for better relationships. Along with these existential crises that questioned the very nature of humanity, twentieth century also witnessed the emergence of the notion of a global village in which distances between nations and cultures shrank, both literally (through migrations) and virtually (by the rapid technological advancements). In other words, religious traditions and religious communities were not as far away as they were previously thought to be—although such multireligious proximity was always existent in pluralistic contexts like South Asia—but rather nearer and closer.

These changes, quite obviously, influenced religions in general, and the church in particular. While there may be several other important developments, there are two watershed events that ushered in a new era in church history with respect to religious diversity in the mid-twentieth century. One was the founding of the World Council of Churches (hereafter, WCC) in 1948, particularly, the formation of the dialogue programme unit, which opened the possibility of conversing with and learning from other faiths. It is pertinent to note here that, predominantly, given their familiarity with religious plurality, it was Christians from South Asia (like P. D. Devanandan, M. M. Thomas, D. T. Niles and Stanley J. Samartha) who inspired and led these programmes on the church's engagement with other religions. Another landmark event pertaining to dialogue was the convening of the Second Vatican Council (hereafter, Vatican II) that met from 1962 to 1964. Notwithstanding their blind spots and shortcomings, as we shall see, the theological basis and directions offered by the dialogue programme of the WCC and Vatican II continue to be as pertinent and helpful as they were more than 50 years ago. It is important to note here that even though our focus is limited to the Protestant church traditions in South Asia, because of their relevance and significance, we will also acknowledge and draw upon the theological wisdom of the Roman Catholic Church in relation to interreligious dialogue. But before we attend to these theological matters, we must first ask, what is interreligious dialogue?

What is Interreligious Dialogue?

Dialogue, as everyone knows, fundamentally refers to conversation, primarily but not exclusively, between *two* individuals or groups. Hence, we may infer that interreligious dialogue is dialogue that happens between two or more religious traditions. At a very basic level, we can say that interreligious dialogue is two or more members from two or more traditions coming together to discuss about their own faith and those of others. However, in order to have a clearer picture of dialogue, I find the following definition offered by East European Protestant theologian Paul Mojzes helpful. Dialogue, Mojzes writes, is

> … a way by which persons or groups of different persuasions respectfully and responsibly relate to one another in order to bring about mutual enrichment without removing essential differences between them. Dialogue is both a verbal and an attitudinal mutual approach which includes listening, sharing ideas, and working together despite the continued existence of real differences and tensions. (Quoted in Race 2008: 156)

Thus, interreligious dialogue is a conversation between religious traditions represented by members of their communities, with a conscious sense of mutual respect, yet without a compromise of their unique features. Because dialogue became popular in the post-Holocaust and post-World War era, it is often mistaken to mean conflict resolution or just a 'strategy' to live with tolerance. But, as the well-known Sri Lankan ecumenical theologian Wesley Ariarajah shows, "[D]ialogue is not so much about attempting to resolve immediate conflicts, but about building a 'community of conversation', a 'community of heart and mind' across racial, ethnic and religious barriers where people learn to see differences among them not as threatening but as 'natural' and 'normal'" (Ariarajah 2012: 14). In that sense, dialogue is more than about being 'tolerant' of the religious 'other' where we learn to 'patch up' or 'put up' with our religious neighbours, but rather an attempt to help people understand and accept the religious 'other' precisely in their "otherness." Dialogue therefore is about relating with the religious others, accepting and cherishing them and their faith as they are, and importantly, learning from them.

Keeping these fundamental elements of interreligious dialogue in mind, what can we say about the aims and assumptions that drive this practice? Douglas Pratt points out that any interfaith dialogue should have a threefold aim (Pratt 2014: 14ff), which, I suggest, also implies the basic assumptions for engaging in dialogue. Firstly, interreligious dialogue should lead to greater respect. There needs to be an attitude of openness to see and accept dialogue partners from other traditions for who they are and what their tradition is. This means that dialogue should *begin* with the assumption that other religious traditions are worthy of respect and dialogue. One cannot expect respect to grow between religions without a basic sense of acceptance among the members of the community. Secondly, Pratt notes that dialogue should lead to the deepening of spirituality. At the end of dialogue there has to be some change at a deeper level within those interacting. This means we have to remember that interreligious dialogue is not simply about abstract texts and statements. It is about the faith commitments and spiritual values of the participants. And when the significance of these commitments and values are borne in mind by those across 'the dialogue table', dialogue can indeed facilitate one's spirituality to be enriched through the encounter. Finally, dialogue should lead to the acceptance and fulfilment of common responsibilities as *a* human family and co-inhabitants of this planet. In other words, we talk not simply because we want to talk but also because we want to live and act together. This awareness and passion to act for change is especially important given the reality of—both human and non-human—suffering that is orchestrated by exploitative social and political structures. To put it differently, foregrounding commitment to justice and liberation of the oppressed is a non-negotiable requirement for dialogue.

Theological Basis for Dialogue

Assumptions and aims of dialogue, as important as they are, can neither be credible nor relevant without addressing the underlying theological suppositions. Since we shall return to this important subject again in other chapters, only a brief argument will be made here. One of the fundamental theological assumptions on which interreligious dialogue is grounded is the basic Christian belief in the universality of divine presence. In other words, God revealed in Jesus Christ is not a tribal or communal God but the source of existence of all that is. This is so precisely captured by the famous theologian Paul Tillich when he suggests that God should be understood "first of all as being-itself or as the ground of being" (Tillich 1973: 235). However, accepting the fact that God is indeed the universal essence of all being(s) should also remind us of the broadness and the deepness of the divine. That is, there is always 'more' to what we can ever see or understand about God. Such unfathomable depth of divine mystery is particularly true when it comes to divine self-revelation.

The Christian tradition strongly believes that God reveals God-self through Jesus Christ. But if we keep in mind the universality and the essentiality of God as the ground of being, we cannot but imagine that when God chooses to reveal herself in this world, it cannot be limited to one instance or even certain instances in human history. In other words, God—understood as the universal source of all that is—must reveal God-self in a plurality of ways. As Ariarajah says, "...given the Christian understanding of God as creator and provider, and the Christian affirmation of the immanence of God, and the Christian conviction that God reveals Godself in history, it should come as a shock and surprise if God's grace and self-revelation are absent in other religious paths" (Ariarajah, 2014: 61). This immanence and the plurality of God's presence become even more explicit if we consider the Trinitarian understanding of God, which is one of the foundational beliefs of the church. The Spirit of God who is also the Spirit of Christ is one who is present and active throughout human history. This is the Spirit who entered the first primordial (human) being, *adam*, energising its body with life. If this is true, can we not say that this life-giving universal Spirit is also active in other religious traditions and their communities? And if it is true that this Spirit is alive and active beyond our familiar (Christian) boundaries, should we not respect and accept the message and value of other religions? And how will we know what they believe and what they have to say if we do not converse with them? Herein lies the theological rationale for interreligious dialogue.

But why should we talk to them? Are we not good the way we are, as a church? Do we not know whatever needs to be known as far as salvation is concerned in Jesus Christ and in his gospel? We need to remember that though the church has the privilege of experiencing the grace of God revealed in Jesus Christ, and (therefore) indeed embodies a reconciled relationship with God, it is still far from perfect. As the Apostle Paul rightly noted, we cannot become overconfident and self-satisfied in the Christian faith. We cannot claim to "have already obtained" perfection or to "have already arrived at the 'goal'," but rather "press on to take hold of that for which Christ Jesus took hold of" us (Philippians 3: 12-14). The prominent ecumenical theologian, Lesslie Newbigin, who was a missionary-pastor and bishop of the Church of South India also echoes the words of Paul when he writes,

I find some Christians are shocked by the suggestion that we have anything to learn from a Hindu or a Muslim at the deepest level of faith. Do we have it all in Jesus? At this level do we not have to teach, to proclaim, to bear witness?

Yes indeed; but also to listen and to learn. It is indeed all there, in Jesus—'all the fullness of God' as Paul says. That is why I must continue to point all men to him as the one true centre around whom the human family can be made one. But I do not yet possess all this fullness. I know in part, but not in full. Even the whole Church does not yet know in full. It has continually to press on toward the fullness of the knowledge of God in Jesus Christ. It can only be at the end, when every tongue confesses him Lord, and when all things have been 'summed up in him' (Eph. 1: 10) that we shall know the fullness of all that he is. (Newbigin 1977: 18)

Therefore, as important as the church is, since she is still in the process of being fully sanctified, we *have* to listen to and learn from other religious communities. In other words, dialogue is not only the need of our times, it is at the very heart of the theological foundation of the Christian tradition.

Types of Dialogue

So far we have looked at interreligious dialogue as a verbal conversation between members of different religious traditions. However, as we know, dialogue between religions can take different forms. Here we follow the popular and well-known classification suggested by the Roman Catholic Church in its document on Dialogue and Proclamation (*Dialogue and Proclamation* 1991).

Dialogue of Theological Exchange: This kind of dialogue generally includes theological and philosophical conversations among scholarly-minded religious representatives. Here members who have a substantial knowledge of their traditions seek to deepen their understanding of their respective religious heritages and appreciate each other's theological convictions. The conversations arranged under the aegis of the World Council of Churches are a good example.

Dialogue of Religious Experience: In this type of dialogue, there is learning and sharing of spiritual practices between religious traditions. Members rooted in their own religious traditions speak and listen to the members of other faiths about their religious practices. We see such experiential dialogues in the form of interreligious prayers organised in ecumenical gatherings, and also during the remembrance of times of crisis (such as the COVID-19 pandemic).

Dialogue of Action: Our world is filled with several unjust and discriminatory structures and systems. In the South Asian context, for instance, we are aware of issues such as poverty, caste, and patriarchy that divide, discriminate, and dehumanise a significant section of the society. While it deepens theological convictions and enriches spiritual values, and is certainly important and valuable, unless interreligious dialogue addresses practices of oppression, its relevance and even its credibility becomes questionable. Taking these concerns into consideration, Christian theologians like Paul Knitter have called for the need for religious traditions to enter into a globally responsible, praxis-oriented dialogue with human and ecological well-being as the common agenda for conversation and action (Knitter 1995: 98–117).

Dialogue of Life: All the different models of dialogue that we have seen until now are deliberately planned and held, often (though not always) at an institutional level. But we know that perhaps the most prominent and powerful way of interreligious engagement happens in 'real life.' That is, dialogues have always been happening, particularly in South Asia, among common people in their day-to-day life experiences. In that sense, we may even say that dialogue between religions is not new after all. In fact, it happens whenever and wherever people strive to live and learn from their fellow religious neighbours with an open and tolerant spirit, sharing their joys and sorrows, their problems and concerns. As we will see below, such dialogical way of living results in the formation of hybrid identities.

Issues in Interreligious Dialogue

Like any idea or practice, interreligious dialogue is not free from shortcomings and blind spots. But thanks to the critical observations made by perceptive scholars, there is a more critical approach to dialogue today. Keeping this in mind, in this section we shall consider some important issues that have been identified in dialogue with respect to the South Asian context.

A.   *Perpetrating and Perpetuating Injustice*

Religions in general are bound to social systems, including those that are discriminatory and oppressive. For instance, we cannot deny the fact that most (if not all) religions have become citadels of patriarchy. As feminist scholars of religions have alerted us, in spite of women being an integral part of all religious traditions and even playing a crucial role in the growth of some of them, their voices have often been silenced and ignored. A good example is Christianity itself, which, in spite of the active participation of women from the time of Jesus, has rather 'conveniently' sidelined and silenced them, with some rare (though notable) exceptions, for the most part of its 2000-year history. This misogyny and androcentrism, quite expectedly, have crept into the arena of dialogue (Ariarajah 1999: 59ff). Another glaring problem has been the indifference and silence regarding caste and untouchability in dialogue, raising the doubt "whether dialogue has not become part of a 'conspiracy of invisibility' which 'refuses to see' and 'deliberately ignores' the issue of the oppression of Dalits and Adivasis under the caste system" (Rajkumar 2013: 166). To these issues we may also include the discrimination against Lesbian, Gay, Bi-sexual, Transgender and Queer communities, and differently abled people, just to name a few, at the dialogue table.

B.   *Elitism*

Another important issue in interreligious dialogue that has been identified is the problem of elitism. Because interreligious dialogue, especially at the global and ecumenical level, involves theological and philosophical musings and deliberations, often it becomes an enterprise that is disconnected from the grassroots realities, and we may add, possibilities. But it is important to note that elite in this book means more than being educated or intellectually inclined. Rather, by elite we (the authors) refer to those who, along with being educated, are also from the higher rungs of society—more often than not male, heterosexual, upper caste, etc.,—and therefore are able to wield power in the church and in society. These privileged voices assume, as Muthuraj Swamy observes, that religious communities are rigidly compartmentalised and, more often than not, live in conflict with each other. Moreover, this sort of elitism also treats the common people as ignorant and valueless and, therefore, worthy only of patronising and nothing more. Therefore, rather than observing and listening to learn how religious communities exist together and resolve their occasional disputes, elite and institutional voices keep working on organising formalised (read, text-oriented and non-people centred) dialogues (Swamy 2016: 148–157).

C.   *Western Imperialism*

Finally, while the initiatives taken by Christians to engage in interreligious dialogue is certainly commendable, we should not ignore the historical connections between Christianity and colonialism. Christianity often supported and legitimised the military expansions of European empires. Even missionaries and mission bodies, except for a very few exceptions, did not question or challenge the violent pursuits of colonialism. Christianity, without doubt, was the privileged religion during the colonial era. No wonder then that, given the continuing Western dominance, there is suspicion whether Christian privilege—albeit usually unintended—becomes translated into projects of interreligious dialogical encounters. In other words, we cannot ignore the fact that Western imperialism is always lurking behind interreligious engagements. This is especially a concern since it is often churches and Christian organisations that set the agenda for dialogue. Therefore, it becomes imperative for dialogue partners, particularly Christians, to acknowledge the power imbalance and their patronizing attitudes when they sit at the dialogue table (Hedges 2010: 96–99).

Living Dialogue: Multiple Religious Belonging

As we note the importance of interreligious dialogue and the different issues involved, there is another form of Christian engagement with other religions that is becoming more visible. This new interreligious trend is known as multiple religious belonging/participation (For more on differences between "belonging" and "participation," see Thatamanil 2016: 9–11; in this book we choose the more popular term "belonging").

Multiple religious belonging (hereafter, MRB) is becoming increasingly popular in the West (Briggs: 2011). In this new trend, double or multiple religious belongers attempt to learn from, participate in, and identify with more than one faith tradition. For example, Paul Knitter, the well-known pluralist theologian of religions, claims that he is a better Christian by becoming a Buddhist. As a committed Catholic he asserts: "My core identity as a Christian has been profoundly influenced by my passing over to Buddhism" and "... the more I have discovered what it really means to be 'in Christ Jesus' the more I have felt the need and the ability to listen to and learn from the Buddha..." (Knitter: 2011: 215–216).

Of course, this is not new to the South Asian context. A good exemplar of multiple religious belonging in the South Asian context is Swami Abishikthananda. Though he continued to identify as a Christian, he acknowledged that he was deeply and profoundly influenced by the *Advaita* Hindu tradition. Despite it being a Hindu concept, Abishikthananda argued that there is "no real contradiction between *advaita* and Christianity" for in every Christian's yearning for a deeper union with the divine, (s)he only discovers that "even the remotest and most inaccessible 'caverns' of his heart turn out to be occupied already, and the darkness in which he had hoped to save his personal existence from annihilation in Being is already ablaze with the glory of God" (Du Boulay 2006: 64–65). Therefore, he called for the need for each religion to transcend itself—including Christianity—so that it can undergo the 'experience of *advaita*' which he believed was "the highest point attainable by man in the contemplation of the mystery of man and nature" (Du Boulay 2006: 120). From these examples we can infer that the integration of different religious paths result from a deep spiritual and intellectual (soul) searching. Such multiple religious belonging happens by choice, where there is freedom for the individual to choose and chart out her faith in a new religious direction. Thus, multiplicity becomes the means for delving deeper into theological questions that otherwise remain unanswered within one's own tradition.

However, as we know, learning from another tradition need not always result in an official initiation into a second religion like in the case of Knitter. For instance, as John Thatamannil observes, there are multiple religious participations that happen at a cultural rather than a religious level, such as Christians practising yoga or Jews engaging in Buddhist meditations where the Christian does not actually become a Hindu or the Jew a Buddhist (Thatamannil 2016: 8). It should also be noted that not all multiple religious belonging happens with metaphysical or existential questions in mind. It could also evolve in the context of an interreligious marriage. Here, the choice to embrace a new religion is made for personal reasons.

As we consider different possibilities for multiple religious belonging, we know that theological or philosophical curiosity or romantic relationships are not always the main reasons. Apart from the 'opted' and 'chosen' multiple religious belonging described above, multiple religious belonging also happens quite 'naturally' and often unconsciously in religiously pluralistic cultures. That is, in such contexts there is a great interweaving of different religions within a given geographical space so much so that these intersections are experienced and embodied by individuals and communities (more often) intuitively. Thatamannil explains that such "…historically deep and complex modes of communal hybridization are rarely matters of individual choice…" where "persons in community over the course of history have evolved complex patterns of religious multiplicity that have an integrity and wisdom that are community sustaining" (Thatamannil 2016: 25).

Apart from the promise and potential it holds, such religious hybridity and multiple religiosity in the global south also alerts us about the politics of the history of religion itself. In the past few decades, postcolonial scholars of religion have identified the evolution of the category of religion in modernity. Brent Nongbri, in his book *Before Religion* where he gives a historical appraisal of the evolution of the category of religion, notes that,

> "…religion does indeed *have* a history: it is not a native category to ancient cultures. The idea of religion as a sphere of life separate from politics, economics, and science is a recent development in European history, one that has been projected outward in space and backwards in time with the result that religion appears now to be a natural and necessary part of our world" (Nongbri 2013: 7).

In other words, religion is not simply a *sui generis* category that existed in human history forever. Nor is it an *essentialised* and fixed identity of human beings that simply takes different names and forms (such as Christianity or Hinduism). As Nongbri shows, though the word 'religion' itself is old and has existed for over 2000 years, it was not used in the same way that we use it today. Religion as an essentialised identifier only evolved and became consolidated after the sixteenth century in the context of the Reformation, the Enlightenment and colonialism (Nongbri 2013: 85). In the words of the renowned anthropologist Talal Asad, "[I]t was in the seventeenth century, following the fragmentation of the unity and authority of the Roman church…. that the earliest attempts at producing a universal definition of religion were made" (Asad 1993: 40). Elsewhere Asad also notes that the construction of religion as a sacred and private human feature is closely related to the development of its "Siamese twin," secularism in the public sphere (Asad 2001: 221). However, in the South Asian context, it is colonialism that played a more critical role in the evolution of religion. As the European empires 'discovered' new lands and people, and wanted to rule them, they realised that they needed to understand the natives better. And one of the ways in which this was accomplished was through 'cataloguing' the colonial subjects based on several aspects, including the important category of religion (Nongbri 2013: 85–131). In other words, religion was created to rule the colonised subjects more efficiently. It is against this background that we find MRB to be disruptive, effectively dismantling and deconstructing oppressive and divisive colonial epistemic and social constructions.

However, when we talk about MRB what we have seen so far is a more positive approach towards religious hybridity, which I choose to name as *horizontal* religious hybridity. One of the problems with such multiple religiosity is that it does not take into account the power dynamics that operate between religious communities. As postcolonial scholars have pointed out, such "cross-cultural 'exchange'... usually implies negating and neglecting the imbalance and inequality of the power relations it references" (Ashcroft, Griffiths & Tiffin 2013: 136). For frequently, if not always, hybridity occurs with deep-rooted power interests and objectives of sustenance. In fact, more often than it is acknowledged, the socially and the politically dominant communities appropriate the cultural and religious values of the subjugated people. It is along these lines that feminist theologian Kwok Pui-lan warns that hybridity, when articulated and practised carelessly, can become an arrogant intrusion into the lives of the colonised people (Pui-lan 2012:

61–64). However, within the reality of power imbalances, the marginalised and the oppressed can also practice hybridity and multiple religious belonging creatively. Homi Bhaba, who is one of the main proponents of this dimension of hybridity (which I prefer to call vertical hybridity in contrast to other aforementioned types), argues that it

> … lays emphasis on the survival even under the most potent oppression of the distinctive aspects of the culture of the oppressed, and shows how these become an integral part of the new formations which arise from the clash of cultures characteristic of imperialism. (Cited by Clarke 1998: 127)

In other words, through hybridity subjugated people appropriate and use the religious and the cultural resources of the dominant (who usually are also their oppressors) as tools of resilience, resistance and liberation. Thus, we can say that MRB holds promise and potential as a critical tool for liberation and emancipation of subalterns in hierarchically structured societies. A classic example of hybridity and multiple religiosity that is liberative can be found among Dalits in India whose religiosity weaves together their own (hi)stories and worldviews with the myths, beliefs and practices of the dominant caste Hindus. Dalits then use this creative hybrid religious framework to counter the oppressive aggression of caste in their respective local contexts (Clarke 1998: 127–130 & Samuel 2016). What is important to note is that such hybrid interaction also happens across religious traditions among Christian Dalits, whose identities are dynamically formed through synergetic interweaving with Hindu Dalit resources (Jeremiah 2013: 165ff). In other words, by drawing from their non-Christian Dalit religious values and rituals, Dalit Christians exercise their resistance to caste.

To conclude, let us recall what we have seen in this chapter so far. First, we looked at the essential features and different forms of Christian interreligious engagement with other religions. We saw that interreligious dialogue is a theologically based practice that is at the heart of the Christian faith. We also noted how interreligious dialogue is not limited to scholarly discussions, but rather happens, perhaps more enthusiastically and relevantly, among the grassroots people. In the final section, we observed that interreligious engagement also happens through multiple religious belonging. Now, in the next chapter, let us look at the various theological approaches of Christians to other religions.

Bibliography

Ariarajah, S. Wesley. *Not Without My Neighbour: Issues in Interfaith Relations.* Geneva: WCC Publications, 1999.

__________. *Your God, My God, Our God.* Geneva: WCC, 2014.

Ashcroft, Bill, Gareth et al. *Postcolonial Studies: The Key Concepts*, Third edition. London & New York: Routledge, 2013.

Briggs, David. "Hindu Americans: The Surprising, Hidden Population Trends of Hinduism in the US." *The Huffington Post*, 4/28/2011. (Accessed on 11/12/2014).

Clarke, Sathianathan. *Dalits and Christianity: Subaltern Religion and Liberation Theology in India.* Madras: Oxford University Press, 1998.

Du Boulay, Shirley (ed.). *Swami Abishiktananda: Essential Writings.* Maryknoll: Orbis books, 2006.

Hedges Paul M. *Controversies in Interreligious Dialogue and the Theology of Religions.* London: SCM Press, 2010.

Knitter, Paul F. *Without Buddha I Could not be a Christian.* Oxford: Oneworld, 2011.

__________. *One Earth, Many Religions: Multifaith Dialogue and Global Responsibility.* Maryknoll: Orbis Books, 1995.

Jeremiah, Anderson H. M. *Community and Worldview among Paraiyars of South India.* London: Bloomsbury, 2013.

Newbigin, Lesslie. *Christian Witness in a Pluralistic Society*. London: British Council of Churches, 1978.

Pui-lan, Kwok. *Globalization, Gender and Peacebuilding*. Mahwah: Paulist Press, 2012.

Samuel, Joshua. "Practicing Multiple Religious Belonging for Liberation: A Dalit Perspective." *Current Dialogue* 57 (December 2015): 78–87.

Swamy, Muthuraj. *The Problem with Interreligious Dialogue*. London and New York: Bloomsbury, 2016.

Thatamannil, John J. *The Immanent Divine: God, Creation, and the Human Predicament*. Minneapolis: Fortress Press, 2006.

__________. "Eucharist Upstairs, Yoga Downstairs: On Multiple Religious Participation" In *Many Yet One: Multiple Religious Belonging*, edited by Peniel Jesudasan Rufus Rajkumar & Joseph Prabhakar Dayam, 5–26. Geneva: WCC, 2016.

Chapter 3

Theological Approaches
to Religious Diversity

In the previous section, we looked at the practical dimensions of Christian engagement with other religions through interreligious dialogue and multiple religious belonging. However, when we speak of interreligious interaction, we know that not all Christians take the same approach. That is, Christians relate to other religions with different attitudes and convictions. And importantly, we need to be aware that these different stances towards other religions are deeply influenced by how we understand God and how we relate to God in relation to our religious neighbours. In other words, Christian interreligious engagement is founded on theological questions. It is for this reason that much of our wisdom on Christian interpretation of and interaction with other religions draws upon the expertise of theologians and scholars within the discipline of theology of religions (also known as theology of religious pluralism or theology of religious diversity). Keeping this in mind, in this chapter, we are going to take a step back, so to speak, and examine the convictions, particularly the theological convictions, behind these different approaches.

Theology of religions, as Paul Hedges notes, "[A]t its most basic level…, involves constructing an interpretation of how Christianity relates to other religions, what the nature of these other religions is, and what may happen to followers of other religions soteriologically" (Hedges 2010: 16). There are four basic categories into which Christian responses to other religions can be framed: exclusivism, inclusivism, pluralism, and particularism. There are two important clarifications to be made here. First, we should note that there are indeed several typologies in theology of religions that attempt to identify the various Christian approaches (For more on typologies, see Hedges 2008: 17–25). Nonetheless, in this book we will focus on the above-mentioned typology which is probably the most well-known and simplest of all. Second, typologies (or even categories) are not monolithic or exhaustive, but rather represent a broad range of views with some basic common features. In that sense, there is overlapping among different approaches, and not to forget, surprisingly vast differences within each approach. Hence, what we actually have and will be looking at are several strands of exclusivisms, inclusivisms, pluralisms, and particularisms with quite a few similarities across boundaries. Keeping these nuances in mind, we will now study each category carefully in terms of their basic beliefs and assertions by engaging with the voices of major proponents of these positions.

Exclusivism

This is seemingly the most popular and common approach in Christian history towards other religions, although, as we shall see, other theological stances have not been absent as well. Nonetheless, exclusivistic Christianity is a dominant, and, in fact, a growing Christian constituency across the world, especially South Asia. In simple terms, those who take an exclusivist attitude claim that Christianity is *the* true faith, and it is only through Christianity that any person can be saved. Though there are differences in the exclusivistic category—there are two broad subcategories that shall be mentioned here—there are some claims that are fundamental to most, if not all, of them.

One of the basic and popular claims within this view is that divine revelation is found only in Christianity. Other religions, even if they have good values and noteworthy teachings, cannot be treated on the same level as the Christian tradition. And though there may be good people who follow these religions, and are probably ethically and morally better than Christians, because they are not part of the Christian fold, they are (unfortunately) lost and doomed for hell's eternal fire. Therefore, the only possible way out for them is to become a Christian. As can be expected, this is the classical (and the predominant, though not the only) missionary approach which can be found even today. All of us, at some point, would have heard some preachers and evangelists declaring this 'truth' about Christianity: that it is *the* only 'true way' to God.

A prominent voice in this camp is that of the great neo-orthodox theologian, Karl Barth, whose voice has influenced the views of most mainline Protestant traditions across the world. However, Barth believed that all religions are fundamentally corrupt which is captured in his famous categorical declaration, "religion is unbelief" (Barth 2010: 300). What is interesting about Barth's assertion is that he does not spare Christianity either. Why? Because, for Barth, Christianity, like all religions, is a human attempt to reach God. Barth writes,

> If man tries to grasp at truth of himself, he tries to grasp it *a priori*. But in that case he does not do what he has to do when the truth comes to him. He does not believe. If he did, he would

> listen; but in religion he talks. If he did, he would accept a gift; but in religion he takes something for himself. If he did, he would let God Himself intercede for God; but in religion he ventures to grasp at God. Because it is a grasping, religion is the contradiction of revelation, the concentrated expression of human unbelief, i.e. an attitude and activity which is directly opposed to faith. (Barth 2010: 301–302)

However, Barth is quick to add that despite its 'failure' as a religion, Christianity still scores a victory (over other religions) in terms of revelation. Barth argues,

> Religion can just as well be exalted in revelation, even though the judgment still stands. It can be upheld by it and concealed in it. It can be justified by it, and … sanctified. Revelation can adopt religion and mark it off as true religion…. There is a true religion: just as there are justified sinners. If we abide strictly by that analogy… we need have no hesitation in saying that the Christian religion is *the true religion*. (Barth 2010: 326, Emphasis mine)

In other words, because it "is the sacramental area created by the Holy Spirit, in which the God whose word became flesh continues to speak through the sign of His revelation," we can indeed declare that Christianity is the only true religion as opposed to others (Barth 2010: 326 & 361). That is, it is the revelation of God in Jesus Christ that makes Christianity the true religion that it is. This view of Christianity as the true religion, notwithstanding its shortcomings, became popular, particularly in relation to religious diversity, through the likes of Hendrik Kraemer who asserted the "discontinuity" between (Christian) 'revelation' and other 'religions,' thus calling for the need for religious 'conversions' (See Hedges 2010: 22). Paul Knitter, in his typology, rightly names this approach as a "total replacement" of existing false religions with the true religion, viz. Christianity (Knitter 2002: 19ff).

However, there are others who can be identified as exclusivists who have a broader view of non-Christian religions. According to the view of these theologians, divine revelation cannot be limited to Christianity. A well-known proponent of this approach is the former bishop of the Church of South India, Lesslie Newbigin (who was mentioned in the previous chapter). Agreeing with Barth that it is God rather than religion that is the church's ultimate focus, Newbigin, however, suggests that the church cannot

> ... attempt to deny the reality of the work of God in the lives and thoughts and prayers of men and women outside the Christian Church. On the contrary it ought to involve an eager expectation of, looking for and rejoicing in the evidence of that work. There is something deeply wrong when Christians imagine that loyalty to Jesus requires them to belittle the manifest presence of the light in the lives of men and women who do not acknowledge him, to seek out points of weakness, to ferret out hidden sins and deceptions as means of commending the Gospel. If we love the light and walk in the light we will also rejoice in the light wherever we find it—even the smallest gleams of it in the surrounding darkness. (Newbigin 1977: 10)

However, irrespective of the presence of divine revelation, exclusivism is clear that it is only through Jesus Christ that we attain salvation. Writing within the depressing context of the two World Wars and the Holocaust, not to mention the disillusionment caused by human attempts to oppose and justify these acts of violence and destruction, Barth felt the urgency to turn to Jesus as the only hope.

> Jesus Christ does not fill out and improve all the different attempts of man to think of God and to represent Him according to his own standard. But as the self-offering and self-manifestation of God He replaces and completely outbids those attempts, putting them in the shadows to which they belong. (Barth 2010: 308)

In other words, though divine revelation is possible in other religious traditions, because the salvation offered by Jesus is available only in Christianity, the former become inevitably useless at best, and evil at worst. It is also in this sense that the church has come to be seen as an exclusively privileged community, as reflected in the famous dictum of Cyprian of Carthage (d. 258) "*extra ecclesia nulla salus*" (outside the church no salvation). Accordingly, the church is considered to be *the* elect community which alone is capable of being saved and attaining eternal life. Though this emphasis on the absolute centrality of the church is generally associated with the Roman Catholic Church (although it is not as dominant since the mid-twentieth century, we shall soon see why), other church traditions—mainline, evangelical, or Charismatic—also in one form or the other, maintain their superiority over other faith communities. Finally and importantly, the Bible occupies a central place in exclusivism. According to this position, it is only through the Bible that God has revealed her will to this world; all other religious texts—written or oral—are false or irrelevant. Though this disposition is not as strong now, the superiority of Christian scripture over other religious scriptures is a view that is still commonly held by many churches.

Inclusivism

Inclusivism is perhaps the popular theological position of most mainline churches with respect to religious diversity today. This approach is certainly more open than exclusivism in terms of recognising divine presence and revelation in other religious traditions. Based on this belief, it is possible to acknowledge that other religions are not evil or useless, but that they do exhibit expressions of God's presence and love, even if in different ways. Nonetheless, this model still insists that the many expressions of the divine in other religious traditions can find perfection only in and through Jesus Christ. Therefore, Knitter is indeed right in calling this the "fulfillment approach" (Knitter 2002: 63ff). However, as in the case of exclusivisms, we have a wide range of inclusivist positions, cautioning us against a monolithic portrayal. All the same, we shall look at some key features that represent this approach.

In his definition of inclusivism, Clark Pinnock notes that in virtue of the all-pervasive creating and sustaining presence of God, God's grace cannot be limited to one group of people, religious or not. He writes,

> Inclusivism believes that, because God is present in the whole world (premise), God's grace is also at work in some way among all people, possibly in the sphere of religious life (inference). It entertains the possibility that religion may play a role in the salvation of the human race, a role preparatory to the gospel of Christ, in whom alone fullness of salvation is found. (Pinnock 1996: 98)

Thus, non-Christian religious traditions and their religious communities are not bereft of God's grace and God's presence, although they only play a "preparatory role" to receive the gospel, a point to which we shall return soon. On the subject of universal divine movement among all the peoples of the world, it is imperative that we recognise the significance of the Second Vatican Council, which offered a paradigm shift in Christianity's stance on religious plurality. The document that came out of the Vatican II, *Nostra Aetate,* declared that

...other religions found everywhere try to counter the restlessness of the human heart, each in its own manner, by proposing "ways," comprising teachings, rules of life, and sacred rites. The Catholic Church rejects nothing that is true and holy in these religions. She regards with sincere reverence those ways of conduct and of life, those precepts and teachings which, though differing in many aspects from the ones she holds and sets forth, nonetheless often reflect a ray of that Truth which enlightens all men. (*Nostra Aetate*, 1965)

This was indeed a huge step for the Catholic Church to open itself to the possibility of other religions as avenues of God's loving presence. Here we should note the role of Karl Rahner, who was not only a major theological influence during the council but an important guide for anyone interested in theology of religions. Based on the fact that grace is universally available and active *a priori* among all people, Rahner asserted that no one was outside the revelatory and the salvific presence of God. In fact, he was so convinced of this "redeeming" and "justifying grace" that he called those outside Christianity "anonymous Christians," a truth that he wanted all those who engaged in missionary activity to keep in mind. He wrote,

From the point of view of dogmatic theology... it cannot be contested... that the act by which justification is appropriated takes place in the power of the habitual grace which is already present... habitual grace which is offered as the condition enabling the subject to act for his own salvation, and which... is logically prior to the free act by which salvation is appropriated in the subject's own personal life... it can be assumed that the preacher of the gospel who seeks to impart faith as an appropriation of grace addresses himself, and must address himself... to an individual who already possesses justifying grace at least as offered, and indeed, it may be, as already freely accepted in an implicit way. The individual concerned would in this sense be an anonymous Christian. (Rahner 1966: 171)

Thus, those who are not Christians and those who are not members of the church, by virtue of having unconditionally received God's grace—which Christian's know and experience as revealed through Christ—are touched and saved by Christ in their own religions. A very generous outlook indeed!

However, as good as other religions can be, they still have to be corrected or at least enhanced through the gospel of Christ. Hence, Rahner concedes that "[E]ven though anonymous Christianity is prior to explicit Christianity… it itself demands this explicit Christianity in virtue of its own nature and its own dynamism…. to be realized in this visible sacramental mode and in the dimension of the Church" (Rahner 1966: 171). That is to say that even if grace enables the possibility of divine revelation and salvation in other traditions, thus making them valid and true, still they need to be 'fulfilled' by the Christian faith; in fact, it is the existence of this anonymous presence of Christ that draws the non-Christian person to Christianity. In that sense, as another Catholic document on the Church's missionary activity, *Ad Gentes,* states,

> … whatever truth and grace are to be found among the nations, as a sort of secret presence of God, this (missionary) activity frees from all taint of evil and restores to Christ its maker, who overthrows the devil's domain and wards off the manifold malice of vice. And so, whatever good is found to be sown in the hearts and minds of men, or in the rites and cultures peculiar to various peoples, is not lost. More than that, it is healed, ennobled, and perfected for the glory of God, the shame of the demon, and the bliss of men. (*Ad Gentes,* 9)

In other words, as we saw in Pinnock's definition, other religions can serve only as preparation and stepping stones to receive and be healed by the Christian message. In the South Asian context, one of the well-known advocates of this fulfilment approach was John Nicol Farquhar. The need for fulfilment or perfection through Christianity is quite apparent: the normative and salvific presence of Jesus Christ. Even if other religions contain expressions of God's saving grace, it is only Jesus Christ who can and ultimately save the members of those traditions, thereby necessitating the need for them to become Christians, or explicit Christians (as opposed to anonymous ones). It is in this sense that inclusivism is often referred as a "Christo-centric" approach.

However, we know that, given the (predominantly) violent history of Christian conversions, and the annihilation and appropriation of non-Christian (read non-European) cultures during the colonial era, terms like anonymous Christians and conversions become problematic, particularly in a sensitive, pluralistic society like South Asia. It is against this background that we find the more dynamic and open Christ-centred approach of theologians like Gavin D'Costa quite helpful. Even while he asserts that "the normativeness of Christ must always be the implicit or explicit criterion when reflecting upon and evaluating the insights from other religions," D'Costa reminds us that "this belief does not preclude the universal workings of the Spirit, which 'blows where it will'" (D'Costa 1986: 135). Because the Holy Spirit, or the Spirit of Christ to be precise, works among all religious communities, Christians should not be surprised to find Christ at work in these communities (in different ways). And this work of the Spirit of Christ means that not only do other religions have much to learn from Christianity, but that Christianity and the church also have a lot to learn from other religions. D'Costa writes,

The values, truth and insights possessed in Christ not only question, but are also enlarged and enriched through meeting people from other religions. The new depth of this Christological criterion is found, not only in terms of sometimes neglected issues such as the value of the impersonal, the place of evil and the importance of the feminine..., but also in terms of the various indigenous forms of expressing Christ's significance and meaning..." (D'Costa 1986: 133)

In other words, because of the presence of Christ and his Spirit in other religions, there is (or at least, should be) mutual learning, and in fact, mutual fulfilment (D'Costa *Meeting*, 128-132). In a similar vein, Jacques Dupuis suggests that because of the universal presence of the Spirit of Christ, Christianity and other religions can complement each other. Even if these workings are different from that which is found in Christianity, Dupuis argues that "God's saving power is not exclusively bound by the universal sign God has designed for his saving action" (Dupuis 1997: 298). However, like other inclusivists, Dupuis does not compromise the uniqueness of Christ, pointing out that "while the Christ-event plays an irreplaceable function in God's design for humankind, it can never be taken in isolation but must always be viewed within the manifold modality of the divine self-disclosure and manifestation through the Word and the Spirit" (Dupuis 207). In other words, even if the Spirit moves among all religious communities, working in a plurality of ways, it always finds meaning only because it is the Spirit of the Word become flesh.

Pluralism

This is the third model in the classical typology of the theologies of religions. In its basic form, the pluralistic approach asserts that divine revelation *and* salvation are not limited to Christianity, but can be found in all religions. Each religion, in its own distinct way, is concerned about and revolves around the same centre, known by different names—God or Ultimate Reality or The Real. In other words, all religions are (only) different human attempts to reach a common goal. At the same time, this common centre or goal does not enforce sameness or integration among religions, but rather allows religions to exist and flourish independently on their own. In that sense, in pluralism there is a "radical openness" among religions (Hedges 2010: 109ff). And, as in the case of the previous two approaches, pluralism consists of a number of positions of which we shall consider two in this book.

One of the most well-known proponents of the pluralist approach is the late British theologian John Hick. Though Hick's thesis has been challenged and critiqued over the years, nonetheless, his framing and naming of the basics of pluralism cannot be ignored by any Christian interested in the subject of religious diversity. Hick's approach is deeply philosophical, particularly based on the works of the Enlightenment philosopher Immanuel Kant. Kant pointed out that when we know or experience any 'thing' (an object or a person) in this world/universe, we always know/understand it only in part, as it is presented to us (what is known in philosophical terms as the thing's *phenomenon*) and not the actual thing itself (*noumenon*) because of various factors (historical, social, political, cultural, etc.). Thus, "what we know is always the thing's *phenomenon*— the image resulting from the way it presents itself and the way our minds process it. We never really, or never fully, know the *noumenon*—the thing in itself" (Knitter 2002: 116). On the basis of this premise, Hick argued that what all religions talk about could only be the *phenomena* (that which is known) of the actual *noumenon*, what he called the 'Real.' Using this philosophical framework, Hick proposed what is famously known as the Copernican revolution in theology of religions. He suggested that all religions are like planets revolving around the sun (i.e. the Real—also addressed as the Ultimate Reality, Ground of Being, Source of existence, Brahman, or simply, God) in different orbits. However, these differences (from the centre) does not make them any less or more valid, but rather should be owed to the limitations of all finite things (Hick 1980: 36). And, what all religions insist is that their constituents strive, in their own distinct ways, to move from a state of self-centredness towards reality centeredness, i.e. to better understand and enter into union with the Real. This means that the salvations offered by different religions, even if expressed differently, ultimately culminate in the Real at the centre. Hence, for Hick, since all religions strive and ultimately attain salvation in God, there is no reason for Christians to look down upon other religions. Because of its insistence on 'God,' this position is believed to foreground 'Theo-centrism' rather than "Christo-centrism."

But what about the Christian belief that Jesus is the saviour of the world? On the uniqueness of Jesus Christ, Hick proposed that incarnation has to be understood metaphorically. That is, instead of saying that Jesus is literally the son of God, Hick suggested that, as stated by the council of Chalcedon, Jesus was both fully divine and *fully human*. This means that Jesus was 'fully' a normal human being—like any other person—but also experienced and expressed God in an extraordinary way (Hick 1973: 154). We should note that Hick is not denying the significance of Jesus. Using the language of *Agape* (divine love), Hick clarifies how he understands Jesus Christ.

> We want to say of Jesus that he was *totus deus,* 'wholly God', in the sense that his *agape* was genuinely the *Agape* of God at work on earth, but not that he was *totum dei,* 'the whole of God', in the sense that the divine *Agape* was expressed without remainder in each or even in the sum of his actions. We want to say that the *agape* of Jesus is the divine *Agape* as this has been acting toward us as an agent within human history. Jesus' *agape* is not a representation of God's *Agape*; it *is* that *Agape* operating in a finite mode; it is the eternal divine *Agape* made flesh, inhistoricised. (Hick 1973: 159)

In other words, Jesus Christ indeed fully embodied God's love in the world in the fullest and the truest possible way just as the church believes. And yet, if we take into consideration the finiteness and the limitations of his human nature and the infiniteness of God (understood in terms of its mysterious and unfathomable depth), Hick, and we may add other pluralists in general, believe that Jesus cannot be an exhaustive revelation of God. In fact, seeing God in Jesus should encourage us to look for revelations in other places and persons.

As convincing and popular as it is, nonetheless, Hick's God-centric or Theo-centric argument has faced several criticisms. As we saw, Hick assumes that there is a common divine centre for all religions. However, as other theologians who engage with religious diversity have shown, this thesis runs into trouble when it comes to non-theistic religions like Buddhism. The seriousness of the impossibility of a common centre can be discerned if we note that it basically created another separate group in theology of religions which we shall see soon. However, among the pluralists, acknowledging this impasse, a new solution was suggested by theologians with a liberationist leaning. A prominent proponent of this pluralist approach is Paul Knitter who proposed that rather than worry about a common divine centre—an undiscernible matter anyways—we should look for a common centre at the human level. As a liberation theologian himself, Knitter argues that it would be helpful if different religions start with the visible concerns of the world such as injustice and suffering. He points out that these could and should become our common focus for dialogue and action. He writes,

> If the religions of the world... can recognize poverty and oppression as a common problem, if they can share a common commitment... to remove such evils, they will have the basis for reaching across their incommensurabilities and differences in order to hear and understand each other and possibly be transformed in the process. (Knitter 1987: 186)

In that sense, what Knitter calls for is not Christo-centrism or Theo-centrism, but rather the centring of the sufferings and the emancipation of the poor and the oppressed. Such a common agenda will help overcome the theological impasse of the Christo-centric and the Theo-centric approaches; after all, all of us, irrespective of our religious background, can relate with the problems of humankind and our planet. Knitter calls this new socially sensitive and responsible/responsive pluralist approach—or ethical-prophetic bridge as he identifies it (Knitter 2002: 134)—*soterio*-centrism. Knitter differentiates the three theological paradigms within pluralism as follows:

> A Christ-centered theology continues to stress the necessity of the church, in relation to Christ; a God-centered view of other religions continues to press the necessity of Christ, but within the trinitarian nature and activity of God. And a salvation-centered approach preserves the value and the necessity of church, Christ, and God as it holds up *soteria* or human and ecological well-being as the context and criterion for a theology and dialogue of religions. (Knitter 1995: 37)

Now, because *soteria*—understood as liberation from unjust suffering—is the overarching framework of relating with other religions, Knitter insists that the emphasis should be on praxis, i.e. action for bringing about practical changes in the world. As a matter of fact, "talking after acting makes for better talking" among religions (Knitter 2002: 139). But is this dialogue of action for justice possible for all religions? Knitter believes so. According to him, religions need not struggle to find some way to be concerned about and work for justice and peace. Rather, he believes that "representatives of all the religions can find within their own traditions, a desire to promote human and ecological well-being and visions of how that might be done" (Knitter 1995: 99). Thus, it is indeed possible for religions, based on their own religious teachings, to acknowledge and work together to alleviate the sufferings of the oppressed and our planet. And, during this dialogue of (social) action, Knitter believes they will be able not only to enjoy harmonious unity but also gain new enriching insights from each other.

But, what about Jesus? Knitter asserts that according to those who advocate an ethical-prophetic form of pluralism, Jesus is "the mystical-prophetic liberator," who like the biblical Jewish prophets, "responded to the sufferings of victims and… called the Jewish people to move their faith in a God of love and justice from empty words to actual practice," thus striving to bring about "the liberation and the transformation of individuals and their social world" (Knitter 2002: 144). And because Jesus himself focused, not on himself, but rather on God and God's reign of justice and peace, Knitter believes that Christians should be concerned about what Jesus taught and how he lived out the values of God's kingdom rather than with the person of Jesus. This shift of focus, pluralists like Knitter believe, would help us and other religious communities to relate and dialogue with each other with mutual confidence and ease. Thus, this praxis-oriented and justice-centred pluralist model can be seen as a more practical and useful way for Christians to relate to other religions.

Particularism

Particularism (or Particularities, as it is also called) is a relatively recent addition to the theologies of religions. Because much of its theological grounding developed out of the other approaches, it is difficult to identify the distinct features of this model. Moreover, to a great extent, particularism was proposed as a critique of and an alternative to the pluralist position. There being several positions within this approach—some of them even overlapping with the other three—let us look at some representative voices.

Pluralism, as we just saw, recognises the validity of all religions based on the fact that they all have some common centres of worship (Real) or common goals of action (justice for the world). However, scholars with a postmodern sensitivity have made us aware of the impossible (and problematic) notion of universal worldviews and metanarratives. These scholars have helped us to identify and respect the cultural and social particularities of religions, especially non-Christian religions, warning us that these differences cannot be simply erased or overlooked. Thanks to their work, we now acknowledge that, generally, when we assume sameness, it is often the projection and imposition of dominant values. And often these 'universal' truth claims are described and explained using a common language and 'grammar.'

Keeping these eye-opening insights in mind, in the theological world, postmodern views with respect to religious diversity came to be expressed in the form of postliberal theology, whose chief proponent was George Lindbeck. Going beyond the liberal agenda of pluralism that saw all religions as one without considering their particularities, postliberal theology called for the need to recognize radical differences among religions. But to understand the particularist view of religious diversity we must first understand the conceptualisation of religion within this school of thought. Lindbeck argues that from a postliberal framework, the real meaning of religion can be understood neither using a "cognitive-propositionalist" approach, i.e. as a set of doctrines, nor using an "experiential-expressive" approach, i.e. as an inner experience of a higher reality (God), but rather as a "cultural-linguistic" reality. Lindbeck describes the cultural-linguistic approach as follows:

> … a religion can be viewed as a kind of cultural and/or linguistic framework or medium that shapes the entirety of life and thought. It functions somewhat like a Kantian *a priori*, although in this case the *a priori* is a set of acquired skills that could be different. It is not primarily an array of beliefs about the true and the good (though it may involve these), or a symbolism expressive of basic attitudes, feelings, or sentiments (though these will be generated). Rather, it is similar to an idiom that makes possible the description of realities, the formulation of beliefs, and the experiencing of inner attitudes, feelings, and sentiments. Like a culture or language, it is a communal phenomenon that shapes the subjectivities of individuals rather than being primarily a manifestation of those subjectivities. (Lindbeck 1984: 19)

That is, religion is like language. Just as we are born and raised in a linguistic system that exists *a priori*, i.e. before us, and not only provides our means of communication but also shapes our worldviews, we are born into our religious world that predates us, and makes us who we are. In other words, one is a Christian by being born and raised in a Christian home and context.

There is a special language a Christian learns along the way that only she can relate to and understand and speak. A Hindu or a Muslim may not understand this Christian language, at least not in the same way as a Christian does. Lindbeck points out that this is also true of other religions.

> In a cultural-linguistic perspective, different religions will have different answers to how they should relate or not relate to others, for they have nothing materially important in common. (Lindbeck 1984: 131)

This means each religion is its own cultural-linguistic world, and therefore, it is not only incorrect, but also arrogant to presume that there is a common culture or language to all religions. This is even more problematic since these 'commonalities' are often proposed by members of Christianity, a tradition which has a violent history of association with European conquests and colonisation. However, Lindbeck does not suggest that there should be no interaction between religions. Rather,

> Christians may receive much that is helpful from them and they from Christians as well as from each other. This, then, is the basis of non-proselytizing dialogue and cooperation that is respectful of the differences between religions. It does not replace evangelization, but is desirable and, in some circumstances, mandatory. Radical diversity of religions in the acceptance model need not entail their isolation from each other. (Lindbeck 1984: 131)

Thus there is conversation between religions but with mutual respect and acceptance and the objective of learning from each other.

What does particularism say about the ends or goals of religions? Also speaking from a postliberal perspective, Mark Heim proposes that each religion has its own ends, its own "salvations" as he calls them. Creatively using the metaphor of peaks and summits to explain the unmatched singularity of religions and their ends, Heim writes,

> … there are several peaks, for the obvious reason that diverse religious fulfillments stand at their own summits, set so within the texture of their own religious traditions and practices. Each of these peaks represents two options: it can be a penultimate stage in relation to salvation or a final end in its own right. These mountains may be *either* purgatorial or final for those that inhabit them…. At the peak, one can pass irrevocably into the specific religious fulfillment, beyond return. As final ends, these fulfillments stand at the top of their own mountains. Each is a separate summit, marking a height of intensification of one type of relation with the divine. This intensification isolates itself from other relations with the divine that have a similar exclusivity.

> Below each summit lies a spur or ridge from which those who taste this fulfillment may pursue another connection. All the summits are linked by such ridges to the Christian mountain. The Christian mountain is one among others, though we might picture it as lower and broader than the others. (Heim 2001: 279)

Each religion therefore is a peak that is climbed by the members of that particular religion to reach the summit, i.e. the ultimate end of that religion. For Christians it will be heaven or eternal life, for Hindus it will be *moksha,* for Buddhists, the end will be Nirvana, and so on. There are also ridges between the peaks through which a person can dialogue with other religions or use to move to another peak (religion). Yet, as long as they are there on one peak, they can only reach *that* corresponding summit. And importantly, each of these peaks can assert its uniqueness and even claim that it is higher than the other peaks. As Heim believes, "[T]here is a purity, an intensity to these ends that truly is distinctive" (Heim 2001: 283). Thus, particularists emphasise the specificities and the uniqueness of each religion—in particular Christianity—over others, even while allowing for dialogue and mutual learning.

What is the Best Model for the Church?

In this chapter, we looked at the different Christian theological approaches towards other religions. We studied systematically, albeit briefly, the four classical Christian positions in relation to religious diversity, viz. exclusivism, inclusivism, pluralism, and particularism, with the help of their respective advocates. Each of these positions have their own pros and cons, and mean much for their particular adherents, a fact we should respect and appreciate.

Nonetheless, without dismissing or degrading other positions, we (the authors) are convinced that pluralism is the best and, in our opinion, the most relevant approach that does justice to our calling as the church, to the Christian gospel which we revere, and more importantly, to Jesus Christ who we follow and worship as our saviour. That is, we believe that it is unbiblical and unchristian to hold that God's liberative presence is confined to one religion, in this case, Christianity. Based on this belief, we intend to encourage and prod the church to become an adventurous pilgrim community and movement that boldly and radically, and at the same time respectfully, ventures out to acknowledge and learn from other religious traditions in order to deepen and enrich its relationship with God in Christ. These interreligious learnings and engagements, we are confident, will help us as the kingdom-community to work along with our neighbours of other faiths to envision and engender a just and peaceful world.

But wait a minute! Is this possible? Do we not claim that the church is the *only* saved community? Do we not believe that only the Bible is God's holy word? Do we not know that Jesus is the *only* way to eternal life? It is to these critical questions that we turn in the next chapter.

Bibliography

Barth, Karl. *Church Dogmatics*. Peabody, MA: Hendrickson Publishers, 2010.

D'Costa, Gavin. *Theology and Religious Pluralism: The Challenge of Other Religions*. Oxford & New York. Basil Blackwell, 1986.

Dupuis, Jacques. *Toward a Christian Theology of Religious Pluralism*. Maryknoll: Orbis Books, 1997.

Hedges, Paul M. "A Reflection on Typologies: Negotiating a Fast-Moving Discussion" In *Christian Approaches to Other Faiths* edited by Alan Race & Paul Hedges. 17–33. London: SCP Press, 2008.

Hedges, Paul. *Controversies in Interreligious Dialogue and the Theology of Religions*. London: SCM Press, 2010.

Heim, Mark. *Salvations: Truth and Difference in Religions*. Maryknoll: Orbis Books, 1995.

Hick, John. *God has Many Names*. London: Macmillan, 1980.

__________. *God and the Universe of Faiths*. New York: St. Martin's Press, 1973.

Knitter, Paul F. *Introducing Theologies of Religions*. Maryknoll: Orbis Books, 2011.

__________. "Toward a Liberationist Theology of Religions," in *The Myth of Christian Uniqueness* edited by John Hick and Paul F. Knitter. 178 – 200. Maryknoll: Orbis Books, 1987.

__________. *One Earth, Many Religions: Multifaith Dialogue and Global Responsibility*. Maryknoll: Orbis Books, 1995.

Lindbeck, George. *The Nature of Doctrine: Religion and Theology in a Postliberal Age*. Philadelphia: Westminster Press, 1984.

Newbigin, Lesslie. *Christian Witness in a Pluralist Society*. London: British Council of Churches, 1977.

Pinnock, Charles H. "An Inclusivist View" In *Four Views on Salvation in a Pluralistic World* edited by John Hick et al. 93–148. Grand Rapids: Zondervan, 1996.

Rahner, Karl. *Theological Investigations*. Vol. 12. Baltimore: Helicon Press, 1966.

Nostra Aetate. Vatican: 1965. http://www.vatican.va/archive/hist_councils/ ii_vatican_council/documents/vat-ii_decl_19651028_nostra-aetate_ en.html (Last accessed May 15, 2018)

Ad Gentes. Vatican: 1965.

http://www.vatican.va/archive/hist_councils/ii_vatican_council/documents/ vat-ii_decree_19651207_ad-gentes_en.html (Last accessed May 15, 2018)

Chapter 4

Rethinking Christian Claims of Exclusivism

In the previous chapter, we ended with some important suggestions. First, we noted that pluralism, with all its complex and interwoven strands, is the best position for the church if it seeks to be a witnessing community in a religiously diverse context. Secondly, it was suggested that there is an imperative need for the church not only to be open to other religions, but also to learn from them. Thirdly, Christian revelation and salvation, as important and life-transforming as they are for those who believe, cannot be considered as ultimate or absolute, but should rather be treated as one among many revelations and salvations in human history. However, as we saw, making these pluralistic claims also prods us to face some crucial questions: If we think that there are many occasions when the fullness of God's revelation was made manifest in the world, then what do we do with our claim and belief that Jesus Christ is *the* one and only saviour? What about the Bible, our holy book which we consider as *the* Word of God, i.e. words through which God continues to communicate with the world? And does this pluralistic view question the primacy of the church as *the* saved community and the sole avenue of salvation? (Note the emphasis on the definite article in each claim.)

In this chapter we will look closely at all these three questions. We will carefully consider the three main assertions that underlie most popular Christian (exclusivist) positions, viz. the primacy of the church, the unparalleled value of the Bible as the Word of God, and the unique identity of Jesus Christ as the universal mediator of salvation. Even as we consider these three claims, we will also point out how a pluralistic view of the church, the Bible and Jesus Christ, as important and foundational as they are, need not deny or delegitimise the truth and the validity of other religious traditions. It has to be noted here that although many of these insights are not new and have been around for some time now, since they are yet to make a profound impact in the life and ministry of the church, it becomes imperative for us to recall and study them. But before we move further, two clarifications are in order here. First, because of the wide range of pluralist positions, in this chapter we will try to consider and interweave them appropriately and draw a viable framework. Second, the fluid boundaries between the different approaches would necessitate the need to move beyond what is conventionally known as pluralism. In other words, in this chapter, we will also draw upon the wisdom of theologians from non-pluralistic positions. Let us now turn to the question of the singularity of the church.

Outside the Church no Salvation?

Even if the claim of the church's exclusive privilege as God's chosen community and the only vehicle of salvation is—or at least was—generally associated with the Roman Catholic Church, we know that all churches, irrespective of their tradition, do make this claim in one form or the other. In fact, even churches with no affiliation to any particular denomination, i.e. those generally called as independent charismatic churches also see themselves as pathways, often the sole pathways, to heaven. Therefore, for those of us in the church who are interested in considering (in considering whether) other religious traditions are genuine avenues of divine revelation and salvation, it is important that we begin by interrogating the church's claim of primacy.

There is no doubt that in the Christian tradition, the church does have a central place. After all, as the early Christians believed, they were the *ek-klesia*, the "called out" people who gathered together regularly to affirm and celebrate their faith in and commitment to Jesus Christ. The New Testament also speaks of the church as the body of Christ, with Christ as the head. Apart from its functional connotation, viz. that the church as the body of Christ is made up of different parts/members, each with its own work (e.g.: I Corinthians 12: 27–31), this metaphor also implies the supremacy of Christ. As Jurgen Moltmann notes, "Christ is the subject of the church" (Moltmann 1977: 6). In other words, in all its reflections and deliberations, the church cannot but always, one way or the other, speak of Christ. The church is under and accountable to Christ, and can never supersede or overshadow him. But, because Christ as the divine mystery cannot be limited to human understanding, we have to agree that there is a lot more that the church cannot understand or embody. Moltmann captures this truth when he says,

> Every statement about the church will be a statement about Christ. Every statement about Christ also implies a statement about the church; yet the statement about Christ is *not exhausted* by the statement about the church because it also goes further, being directed toward the messianic kingdom which the church serves. (Moltmann 1977: 6)

A few important things have to be noted here. First, the church and Christ are intrinsically related to each other, and as we saw, the church is subordinate to Christ. Second, the church does not exhaust who Christ is and what he represents. To assume that the church knows all about Christ, the human incarnate of the divine, is not just ignorance, but also arrogance and worse still, idolatry. Third, Moltmann reminds us that what we say about Christ goes beyond what we say about the church, especially since Christ was concerned about the much more important reality of the reign of God (also known as the kingdom of God). This means two things. First, the church and the reign/kingdom of God, though related, are not identical. Second, the church is called to serve this larger, deeper, and greater reality of God's reign which Jesus ushered in through his life, death, and resurrection.

This acknowledgment of the nature of the relationship between the church and the reign of God is very important. For a long time, the church was obsessed with itself, i.e. about its own importance and significance in human history. However, since the mid-twentieth century, both the Catholic Church and the Protestant Church have recognised the problem with this approach. In the World Council of Churches, there was a slow but discernible shift from church-centrism to kingdom-centric emphasis (Newbigin 1980: 1–17). Similarly, the Roman Catholic Church also began to move towards acknowledging the primacy of the kingdom of God over the church (Knitter 1996: 108).

But before we look at the importance of the kingdom over the church, we must first ask the question: what is the kingdom of God? Though there may be many ways to define it, we find the Roman Catholic theologian Edward Schillebeeckx's definition concise and helpful. He writes,

> The kingdom of God is the saving presence of God, active and encouraging, as it is affirmed or welcomed among men and women. It is a saving presence offered by God and freely accepted by men and women which takes concrete form above all in justice and peaceful relationships among individuals and peoples, in the disappearance of sickness, injustice and oppression, in the restoration to life of all that was dead and dying. The kingdom of God is a changed new relationship (*metanoia*) of men and women to God, the tangible and visible side of which is a new type of liberating relationship among men and women within a reconciling society in a peaceful natural environment. (Schillebeeckx 1990: 111–112)

Therefore, the kingdom of God is basically the active presence of God among a community that is repentant, reconciled, and liberated from their sufferings. And it is precisely because of its 'perfect' nature, that it is a realised *eschatological* reality, that is, something that exists but will only attain its full potential in the end of history. But why is this kingdom of God more important than the church? To put it simply, the kingdom of God comes from Jesus himself. Drawn from his Jewish religious heritage, the kingdom of God figures as the central theme among Jesus's teachings. In fact, the two—Jesus and the kingdom of God—cannot be separated. Schillebeeckx notes that the concept (of God's kingdom) itself "has to be defined… in terms of the life of Jesus" (Schillebeeckx 1990: 112). In a similar vein, Newbigin warns us that "when the message of the Kingdom is divorced from the Person of Jesus, it becomes a programme or an ideology…," devoid of its actual power and distracted from its original purpose (Newbigin 1980: 18). Therefore, any message or reflection about the kingdom is not only from, but also inevitably about, Christ, and in that sense is of greater importance than the church.

However, though the church and the kingdom are different and the kingdom supersedes the church, it does not mean that the church does not have any significance. As Newbigin asserts, the church "is the community that has begun to taste (even only in foretaste) the reality of the Kingdom" and "can alone provide the hermeneutic" of its message (Newbigin 1980: 19). That is, it is through the church that we are able to interpret and understand the reign of God. We should agree with Newbigin that the church, in that sense, is indeed privileged as the chosen and the called community to be a witness to the kingdom. Nonetheless, the church, as important as it is, cannot become self-centred, but rather should remain under the shadow of the kingdom. As the Indian theologian Michael Amaladoss elucidates,

> It [the church] is called to a twofold service; one is to witness to the Kingdom and to promote its realisation in the world; another is to proclaim Jesus and to build up a community of disciples. *The second is a means of serving the first.* In doing the first service the Church discovers that the mystery of God is active everywhere, in various ways. It has no claims to exclusivity. It discovers a community of faith. It is called to dialogue and to collaborate. It makes its specific contribution to the integral wholeness of the Kingdom. (Quoted in Knitter 1996: 109)

In other words, by committing itself to work for the kingdom—rather than itself—the church's eyes are opened to the truth that God is active in places beyond itself particularly in other religious traditions. Knitter reminds us that, thus, "in a Kingdom-centered orientation of the church and mission, other religions are not only 'ways of salvation,' they are, more precisely and more engagingly, 'ways of the Kingdom' (*viae Regni*)" (Knitter 1996: 118). Therefore, even as we claim and celebrate our privileged status as the church, 'the called out community of God,' we also know that we are not the ultimate community. That honour goes to the kingdom of God, the community of communities that experiences God's loving and liberating presence in diverse ways. This means that we cannot assert that "outside the church there is no salvation," for we know that the divine Spirit is actively present in ways that we cannot even comprehend in order to bring all humanity (and creation) into a deeper union with the source of life and the ground of our being—God.

Is Bible the Only Word of God?

The second important claim that is made to assert the uniqueness of Christianity is that the Bible is the only sacred text that can be considered as the Word of God, meaning that the sacred texts of other religions cannot be considered as sacred or true. More often than not, members of the church believe that other (religious) scriptures are mere stories and myths with no truth or value in them. By contrast, it is claimed that whatever the Christian scripture says is absolutely and literally true. And even those who do not engage in literalist interpretations feel that the sacred books of our religious neighbours really have nothing substantial or useful to offer, and that it is the Bible that is *the* sole text through which God communicates with the church and the world, and "the rock-bottom guide to all that a follower of Jesus does and claims" (Knitter 2002: 22).

Even as we respect such beliefs among Christians, in this book we want to argue that God not only speaks through the Bible but also through other religious texts. That is, God's will and purpose for humanity is not only communicated through the pages of the Christian holy book, but also through the several sacred texts of our non-Christian friends and neighbours. Simply put, the Bible is not the only Word of God; all scriptures—both written and oral—are 'Words of God.'

But how is this possible? On what basis can we make this claim? First, we should remember that all scriptures arise out of the faith experiences of religious communities. As Samartha says,

> The scriptures of any religious group are the objectification of the faith experience of that particular community. Therefore, scriptures have to be regarded not as an absolute creation, but an actualization, a re-creation of the experience. Inspiration can be meaningful only in the context of the faith experience of the believers. (Samartha 1991: 72–73).

In other words, scriptures are the verbalisation of the responses of the faith community to their experience of relating to God or an ultimate concern. This means that the Bible, the Word of God for Christians, is also basically a collection of words about how God relates with and what God does for the world *as historically construed by the Christian community*. And, as Francis Clooney points out, "[T]he intellectual and affective dimensions of relationship to God are accessible through words, in language" (Clooney 2010: 115). However, we know that words that mediate God's presence and will are only finite human efforts to understand, speak about, and experience God. Since (human) language and words can only communicate so much of the depths and riches of divine mysteries, these limitations are also applicable to the Bible. In other words, as important as the words of the Bible are, we know that there is always more that evades and transcends words, especially when it comes to speaking about God. As Samartha reminds us, in general "[L]anguage of religion" which includes both texts and rituals "are not an end in themselves but point to something beyond that is deeper, larger, and more mysterious" (Samartha 1991: 74). Hence, the Bible too, as a sacred text, is not the absolute truth in itself but that which directs and helps us to understand and experience *the deeper Truths of the divine*.

The second reason for disclaiming exclusivist privilege for the Bible comes from the Bible itself. One of the fundamental and mandatory assertions of the Bible is monotheism—that God is one. Throughout all its books, in spite of the vast timeline and the complexities and ambiguities, the Bible uncompromisingly insists on the fact of monotheism. This means that the God of the Bible is not a 'tribal god,' but rather the God of all people. This also means that God is not limited to those people for whom it is the sacred text. Rather, God speaks, hears, and cares for all people wherever and however they may be—this is important—in their own language. Hence, we can say that God is present or active in other religious communities as well. This is precisely why we noted earlier that the kingdom of God transcends the boundaries of the church. Based on this fact, from a Christian perspective, we can say with confidence that because the (one) God of the Bible is active everywhere and relates to people in different ways, their language and vocabulary which express that relationship are certainly valid. Therefore, as Samartha categorically states, "[T]here is indeed a *plurality* of scriptures. This is a fact of history to be accepted, not a theological point to be discussed" (Samartha 1991: 73).

This means that Christians should keep two things in mind with respect to the Bible and religious diversity. Firstly, in order for the Bible to symbolise the truth about God, it has to be continuously reinterpreted according to the context. For,

> … scriptures should not be regarded as "petrified texts" written once for all, or that the entire religious life of humankind is limited to a continual hermeneutical exercise seeking to interpret texts handed over from the past. That would amount to ignoring the leading of the Spirit into new realms of truth and blocking the possibilities of new insights being recognized to sustain life on the way. (Samartha 1991: 74-75)

The message of the Bible is never complete in itself nor is it fixed in time. It is only by reading and rereading the words of the Bible in dialogue with the present context that we would be able to understand their true meaning.

Secondly, because the Bible (and, in fact, all religious texts) are only limited expressions of faith, and because we acknowledge the fact that the knowledge of God's revelation is present in all religious traditions and communities, there is no reason why we should limit ourselves to our sacred text. In other words, we can know about God not only through the Bible but also through other religious texts, even if we do not belong to that religious tradition. This means, we can engage in studying and learning not only the Bible and other Christian texts but also the texts of other religious traditions. Here, a caveat is in order. While learning the texts of other religions, we have to be careful not to 'use'—or, in fact, 'abuse'—the scriptures of other religions by trying to force our interpretations or assimilate them into our religious framework. Rather, studying other religious texts should be done with humility and respect, both towards our own tradition and the one that we engage with. It is worth noting that this interreligious and comparative learning has been explained and attempted by many South Asian theologians like Raimon Panikkar, A.J. Appasamy, to name a few (See, Panikkar 1981and Appasamy 1931). In recent times, these multireligious learning ventures have been made popular through the academic discipline of comparative theology in the West (See Clooney 2010 & Fredericks 1999).

Is Jesus the Only Way?

So far we have looked at how Christian claims of exclusivity with respect to the church and the Bible are not only unnecessary but are also against our very foundational beliefs. We saw that God's salvific presence is available to and in all religious communities, and God reveals her will through the sacred texts of those traditions. But, as we know, there is yet another assertion, important and fundamental—in fact, more important and fundamental—than the others, viz. Jesus is the only way to God and eternal life. In other words, the church believes (based on the Bible) that Jesus is the only saviour of the world. But, when we embrace religious diversity, should we question this claim? Can we say that Jesus is *not* the only way of salvation? Can we suggest that God saves through other people and other means that may not have anything to do with Jesus at all?

Keeping these questions in mind, in this section, we will explore whether there can be valid means of salvation in other traditions without diluting or compromising our belief in the uniqueness of Jesus Christ. We will begin by re-viewing the dynamic relationship between belief and practice. Next, we will look at Jesus's own life and ministry and what his priorities and objectives were. Thirdly, we shall turn to the claims of exclusivity in relation to Jesus and inquire why and how these claims came to be. Recapitulating on these findings, finally, we will try to understand what the uniqueness of Jesus could mean in a multireligious context like South Asia.

To begin with, before we investigate the question of the uniqueness of Jesus Christ and his identity as the only saviour of the world, we must bear two things in mind. Firstly, when we speak of doctrinal statements, such as 'Jesus is *the* way to God,' we should note that these assertions were not the starting point of Christianity. That is, when Christianity bloomed at the dawn of the Common Era, it did not begin with dogmas prescribed and taught by the church leadership. Rather, doctrines arose out of the faith experiences of the believing community. In other words, the Christian faith statements were shaped by the experience of the early Christians over a long period of time, before it took the dogmatic form we see today. In fact, as Katheryn Tanner reminds us, these dogmas are never completely finalised, but rather are continuously being shaped according to the changing times, so much so that we have to see Christianity not as a monolithic community, but rather as "a genuine community of argument" (Tanner 1997: 124).

This is extremely important since we often think and act as if some beliefs of the church, including those professed in the form of the creeds, were written down at a single moment in history, at one go, by some sort of a core planning committee! Yes, it is true that the apostles, and later on the Church Fathers (and not to forget, the Church Mothers) definitely played a crucial role in shaping the beliefs of the church. But what should not be forgotten is that what they believed in and spoke about was shaped by their own and their (wider) community's faith, and importantly, practice. As Knitter perceptively notes, "creedal or orthodox statements... and... confessions of faith (*lex credendi*) grew out of and were meant to nourish the practice of faith in devotion (*lex orandi*) and discipleship (*lex sequendi*)..." (Knitter 1996: 67). In other words, faith practices of the believing community precede and supersede the dogmatic beliefs of the church. Therefore, we need to be careful about making doctrinal statements absolute and final in themselves. Doctrines have always emerged and evolved from and within the experiences of the people.

This importance of 'orthopraxis' (right practices) shaping orthodoxy (right belief) is perhaps nowhere more evident than in Christology (the theological exposition of the life and work of Christ) itself. It is true that we often paint a monolithic picture of Jesus Christ, forgetting that there are a plethora of images that have evolved over the years in Christian history. And when we turn to the Bible and the early church history, a careful reading will show us that there was no one Christology but rather several Christologies. As Schillebeeckx rightly states, "from the first the significance of Christ could only be apprehended by a diversity of formulations" (cited by Knitter 1996: 178). While we cannot mention all these Christologies here, and surely not in detail, we can identify, as Knitter does, four major Christological trajectories in the early church from which sprouted other Christologies: 1) Maranatha or Parousia Christologies which spoke of Jesus as the future judge and king of all creation, 2) 'Divine man' Christology that saw Jesus as a person of God who was able to do supernatural acts, 3) wisdom and logos Christology that served as the seed for pre-existent and incarnational Christologies, 4) Paschal or Easter Christology that emphasised the death and resurrection of Jesus (Knitter 1996: 176–177; For a more detailed study of New Testament and classical Christologies see, Haight 1999: 152–184 & 244–272). Of course, this is only a broad typology, and there are several Christologies, such as Spirit Christology that overlaps with many of the above categories. But, what is to be remembered here is that the reason for the existence of such a rich (and complex) plurality was because these Christologies developed according to the historical context and the needs and experiences of the people in the context. In other words, Christology in the New Testament and the early church period evolved *in*—and in fact *as*—faith experiences/practices of the faith community through an "implicit dialogue with the philosophical, religious thought and experience of the time" (Knitter 1996: 178).

Keeping this in mind, let us now try to re-view the exclusive claims about Jesus. But, if we are going to talk about Jesus, it is only appropriate that we begin with the person himself, Jesus, and what he said (about himself). Of course, we acknowledge that we do not know everything about Jesus's life; only a few moments of Jesus's life are portrayed in the gospels. But nonetheless, what we do know in the gospels are quite sufficient for us to be aware of some important facts about Jesus.

Firstly, we know from the gospels that Jesus's focus during his ministry was not on himself but God. Throughout his life, even on occasions when he spoke of himself, the ultimate focus was (on) God. It is because of this total dedication and deep love that he called and related to God as his *Abba*! We need to remember here is that this focus on and close relationship with God did not come from just anywhere but from his Jewish faith which emphasises on monotheism. It is often forgotten, though this view has been critiqued in the recent past, that Jesus was, throughout his life, a Jew. This means that whatever Jesus spoke and did, because of his religious background, he always glorified (the one) God, the creator and sustainer of all that is (For more on Jesus's Jewish understanding of God, see, Haight 1999: 88–118).

Secondly, we also see in the Gospels that Jesus was deeply committed not to establish his own rule but the reign of God. In fact, we see that Jesus escaped from the scene when people were seeking to anoint him as a king (John 6: 15). It is quite evident that his one and only assignment in life was to usher in and build God's kingdom on earth. No wonder then that we see in his first ministerial proclamation, and repeatedly in his teachings and his many parables, the theme of God's kingdom being emphasized. But what is also significant of this divine kingdom was the objective and its scope. Drawing from his Jewish roots, Jesus spoke of a kingdom that was a community of justice and peace that included everyone as God's children. And as we saw earlier, because of its almost idealistic nature, Jesus described it as an eschatological reality, i.e. as something that will come to fruition at the end and culmination of time. Nonetheless, as Haight elucidates, the kingdom of God which Jesus envisioned,

> … even though it encompasses the end-time, is not something utterly other-worldly, because it points to God acting in history. God's divine power has its effects in history. The kingdom of God, insofar as it points to God's saving power, rights the wrongs and negates the negations of historical reality. (Haight 1999: 98)

Thirdly, Jesus considered himself a prophet, and to be more precise, a millennial prophet who ushered in a new era in human history. We see evidences of this not only in the words of Jesus but also his followers. Hearing his teachings and seeing his deeds, his contemporaries often considered him to be a rabbi (a teacher), but more importantly and influentially, a prophet of God. Once again, we need to see this identity of Jesus within the context of his religious background, particularly the framework of prophecy in the Old Testament (The Hebrew Bible of the Jews). Prophets were not, as it is sadly thought today, predictors of the future or fortune tellers. Rather, they were spokespersons for God who, empowered by the divine Spirit, saw and interpreted the signs of their times diligently and warned or comforted people as the need may be. We see this prophetic dimension of Jesus's life brought out clearly in the Gospels (e.g.: Matthew 24, Mark 13, Luke 21). But, Jesus was also no ordinary prophet; Jesus was an eschatological prophet, someone who felt that he was "the final prophet (Deut. 18: 15–19) who was anointed specially by God's Spirit to complete the mission of the earlier prophets by announcing and enacting the good news of God's final rule" (Knitter 1985: 174).

But, was Jesus not more than these identities? Is he not believed to be the revelation of God in and through whom salvation is offered to humanity? Yes indeed! Jesus surely does stand at the centre of the Christian faith as the perfect mediator and channel of divine revelation and salvation. Another way of putting this is to say that "though subject to individual and social conditions his human spirit was entirely grasped by the Spiritual Presence… or, to use another figure, 'God was in him…'" which "makes him the Christ" (Tillich 1963: 144). In other words, he was so fully filled by the Spirit of God that he was seen and experienced as the embodiment of God herself. Yet, as we saw earlier, Jesus, as human, was always concerned, not about himself but about revealing God to the world. That is to say that Jesus always pointed towards, or to better state it, 'symbolised' God.

Symbols, it should be noted, especially in the religious sense, do not simply point towards an object, in this case, God; then it would become a sign. Rather, religious symbols both *point to* and *participate in* the object of concern. Therefore, we say that Jesus as symbol both directs us towards God and at the same time himself is God (to whom he points). He mediates and directs us towards God, but at the same re-presents God in himself. He simultaneously signifies and enfleshes God in his own self. This is precisely why his followers and subsequent believers (like us) see and worship Jesus as God. But having said that, we should also be aware that a symbol does not and cannot exhaust what it points to. In that sense, Jesus in his incarnational form, as much as he shows who God is to us in and as himself, he also gently reminds us that there is more to the picture, that there is the larger, deeper and infinite mystery that is God which cannot be captured by words or anybody—any 'body.' This is precisely why we (have to) acknowledge and believe—if we remember that Jesus is God's symbol—that believing in Jesus as divine revelation and our saviour does not preclude God from acting to save beyond Jesus. It is in this sense that we are able to say that Jesus is one among many other saviours of the world.

But wait a minute! Does the Bible not say that Jesus is the only way to God? Did not the early Christians, for instance, assert that "There is salvation in no one else, for there is no other name under heaven given among mortals by which we must be saved" (Acts 4: 12)? How can such claims be taken lightly? There is no doubt that these are important belief statements that can be found in the New Testament. Yet, as it is the case with the rest of the Bible (or any religious literature for that matter) we should be mindful of the context of these exclusivistic affirmations. Here we highlight only three major factors that inspired these claims. Firstly, the first century context in which Jesus lived was predominantly a context of eschatological and apocalyptic expectations. That is, tired of years of colonisation by several empires, including the Roman Empire, the Jewish people of the time were hoping for and expecting a drastic shift in the trajectory of history. They anticipated a new era in which God would be in control and Israel would be restored. Therefore, when the first Christians, who were mostly Jewish and were also expecting "a new and definitive stage of history," saw the life and work of Jesus, they came to "the spontaneous conclusion that… this stage had arrived" through his ministry (Knitter 1985: 183). There was no one else to expect further to usher in this new era in history (*kairos*). And even after Jesus's earthly ministry, these early Christian communities believed that he was going to return soon, and therefore, history was wrapping up. Hence, the language of 'only' in the New Testament. In other words, what we see in the exclusivistic statements is the language of 'ultimacy' and 'urgency' since the world as they knew it was coming to an end, and the early Christians wanted everyone to be on board.

Secondly, the claims about Jesus in the New Testament were made in the political and religious context of the Roman Empire. While in general (on the surface) it looked as if the Roman Empire would not disturb the religious beliefs of its subjects, minority communities like Christians were not free of threat. Looming large over them was not only the parent Jewish religion which wanted to maintain a (generally) non-inclusive stance, but also the Greco-Roman religion which directly and subtly affirmed the 'lordship' and divinity of the Emperor, using it to exploit the vulnerable. Both these positions were unacceptable to the followers of Christ, who wanted to be an inclusive and just community. Therefore, in order to avoid being assimilated or stomped out by these larger and powerful religious groups, the early Christians had to use some 'tough' language to assert their distinctiveness. As Knitter notes, "the community had to arm itself with clear identity and total commitment. It did this especially through its beliefs, particularly its Christological beliefs," i.e. beliefs about Jesus Christ (Knitter 1985: 184).

Finally, we need to know that the statements about Jesus were made out of deep devotion and intimate experience with him. That is, the claims about Jesus as the one and only saviour were made by people who were very close to him and were fully committed to him. Krister Stendahl rightly notes that what the disciples and the early Christians used to describe Jesus, especially in the Gospels and other New Testament books, was "love language" or "caressing language" (Cited by Knitter 1985: 185). To understand this, imagine a couple who are in love with each other. In such a loving and intimate relationship, one of the partners might declare to the other (as many of us would have done): "You are the most beautiful person in the world; there is no one as attractive and good-looking like you!" Of course, the one who says this certainly means what she says, in the sense, *in her eyes*, the other person is certainly the loveliest person in the whole world! And yet, we know that empirically and realistically, this is far from true. Just because we think that our partner or spouse or the person we love is the most beautiful person in the world does not mean that this is literally true; certainly there are other people who would be more beautiful than our partner, not to forget that beauty is a relative matter. This is exactly what happened in the case of Jesus. Jesus, *for* his followers and those who believed in him, was certainly and surely the way of receiving and experiencing God's salvation. Note that the emphasis is on 'for.' This means that what is true for those who believe in Jesus is indeed true and worthy of being shared—the early Christians were indeed doing this—but that does not and cannot mean that it is the universal and absolute truth and fact for everyone. For others, there might be other 'beautiful' people, other 'only ways' to experience salvation and reconciliation with God. Love language of the Bible, therefore, cannot and should not be universalised.

It is clear that we obviously do not live in the above-mentioned circumstances. While the message of Jesus is true for all ages and should be considered as normative, we do not have to be bound to and governed by the necessities of the first century context. Our religiously pluralistic South Asian context invites us to re-view and reinterpret the life and the message of Jesus dynamically. Therefore, keeping these facts in mind, we can arrive at three conclusions regarding claims of exclusivity for Jesus as the only saviour of the world. First, we do not have to compromise who Jesus is for the church, the incarnate one who reveals God and mediates divine salvation to us. But, what is also important for us is not just to believe in him but also to follow his way of love and justice. Second, as important as Jesus is for us, we need to accept that he does not, as God's human incarnation, exhaust or entirely (re-)present who God is. Therefore, we can say that indeed there are different ways in which others experience divine revelation and salvation. In other words, Jesus is one of the many revelations and salvific mediations of God. Of course, here we should be aware of the criticisms that we saw posed in the earlier chapter in regard to imagining a single/common divine centre or goal (often identified as God) to all religions. In fact, some religions like Buddhism do not have a concept of (a single creator) God at all. There is, in fact, the possibility of more than one ultimate reality (Cobb 1999: 184–185). Nevertheless, we can agree, from a Christian perspective and in relation to the issue of Christian exclusivist attitude, that Jesus Christ is not and cannot be the only one who helps human beings to relate with and experience the ultimate and deeper realities of existence. Thirdly, when we realise that Jesus is not the only way to God, we are able not only to respect other divine instantiations in human history but also to learn from them. These divine revelations are after all alternative ways to God. Therefore, in conclusion, we can say, "Yes! It is possible for us to be committed to our Lord Jesus Christ, and yet at the same time, acknowledge, celebrate, and learn from the instantiations of the divine in other religious traditions and communities!"

Bibliography

Appasamy, A. J. *What is Moksa? A Study in the Johannine Doctrine of Life.* Madras: CLS, 1931.

Fredericks, James L. *Faith among Faiths: Christian Theology and Non-Christian Religions.* New York/Mahwah: Paulist Press, 1999.

Panikkar, Raimundo. *The Unknown Christ of Hinduism: Towards an Ecumenical Christophany.* Maryknoll: Orbis Books, 1981.

Haight, Roger. *Jesus: Symbol of God.* Maryknoll: Orbis books, 1999.

Clooney, Francis X. *Comparative Theology: Deep Learning across Religious Borders.* Chichester: Wiley-Blackwell, 2010.

Samartha, S. J. *One Christ–Many religions: Toward a Revised Christology.* Maryknoll, NY: Orbis books, 1991.

Newbigin, Lesslie. *Sign of the Kingdom.* Grand Rapids: William B. Eerdmans, 1980.

Schillebeeckx, Edward. *Church: The Human Story of God.* New York: Cross Road, 1990.

Cobb, Jr., John B. *Transforming Christianity and the World: A Way Beyond Absolutism and Relativism.* Maryknoll: Orbis books, 1999.

Moltmann, Jurgen. *The Church in the Power of the Spirit.* New York: Harper and Row, 1977.

Knitter, Paul F. *No Other Name? A Critical Survey of Christian Attitudes Toward the World Religions.* Maryknoll: Orbis books, 1985.

————. *Jesus and the Other Name: Christian Mission and Global Responsibility.* Maryknoll: Orbis Books, 1996.

Tillich, Paul. *Systematic Theology* Volume III. Chicago: The University of Chicago Press, 1963.

Chapter 5

Listening to Silenced Voices: Ethical Norms for Interfaith Dialogue and Action

In the previous chapters we discussed how interreligious dialogue (hereafter IRD) is a theologically based practice. We, as authors, have maintained that a pluralistic approach to mission and evangelism is the best option for the church. The Christian interest in other religions is not new. The missionary conferences in Edinburgh 1910, Jerusalem 1928, and Tambaram 1938, have taken serious note of other religions. The New Delhi assembly of the World Council of Churches in 1961 referred to dialogue as a form of evangelism which is effective even today (Samartha 1981: 2). In subsequent assemblies, the importance of dialogue was continually stressed. In short, dislocating from missionary theology and developing a favourable theology of religions in a plural context through dialogue has special significance. Dialogue has been included in the ecumenical agenda because the ecumenical movement is concerned with the "whole inhabited world," including those who are part of one human family that adhere to another religion (Kinnamon

& Cope 1997: 394). Therefore, the concern for dialogue goes beyond geographical locations and takes place within the concrete life of human beings.

In the South Asian context especially, we see pluralism in religions, cultures, customs, languages and worldviews amid widespread economic inequality. The plurality of religions and cultures in South Asia is a gift too. However, we have not been able to make the best out of this gift because of the antagonism between religions.

South Asia is a land of diversities, and all kinds of religions exist here; the fact is that all religions do not work for the same objectives. These religions are based upon different understandings of God, humans, nature, and purpose of creation. For most people, religion serves as an assurance of happy personal existence after physical death (Rao 1991: 81). However, there are others whose main interest in religion is the intellectual satisfaction they find in the deep pursuit of the universal truth. There are still others for whom religion means psychological or emotional fulfilment or even a mystical experience. And there are those for whom the main value of religion lies in its provision of a moral code by which they can improve the quality of their lives and even strive towards ethical perfection. Religion means different things to different people. Since people are different their emotional and psychological needs too are different. It therefore becomes important for us to understand other religions so that we are more responsible in our communications with them. An IRD is a platform for enhancing our understanding of other religions. Since IRD is a part of the daily life of people in South Asia, it also becomes a tool to understand how people have been interacting so as to overcome divisions.

Consequently, understanding another religion is not the sole motive of IRD. Dialogue is not an intellectual pursuit towards understanding dogmas and doctrines of other religions. In South Asia, dialogue is about people and their concerns, and tackling poverty is one of the greatest challenges. Conversations on poverty bring forth issues of injustice, unequal sharing of resources, marginalisation and oppression. The widening gap between the poor and the rich, free-market economy, and mushrooming of foreign direct investments that push the poor to the extreme and damage their social, political, economic and religious life. In such contexts we need to ask questions to find a purpose and meaning of religion. What is the purpose of religion? How do we enhance the life of the community? How can we work against the unjust structures in society? How can we liberate humanity from suffering and bondage? How can we empower the oppressed classes who have been so for centuries? How can we relate our faith to action? These questions are significant because theology cannot neglect the human situation. Interreligious cooperation thus becomes fundamental to issues pertaining to justice, peace and love. In a deeper sense, as Israel Selvanayagam says, "Dialogue implies intimacy of personal relationship, enjoyment of each other, and sharing of knowledge, experience, problems, suffering and resources" (Selvanayagam 1995:2). In addition, as Anthoniraj Thumma points out, "The focus of dialogue should be to foster reciprocal communication in order to seek truth, to grow in love, nurture peace, enhance freedom, and promote life and liberty for all" (Thumma 2000: XII). IRD is thus a call for religions to come together to fulfil a common interest for peace, justice and liberation.

At the heart of dialogue is sharing for spiritual and historical experiences and searches for a just and loving community.

Methodologically, we thus have to move from *plurality of religions* to *plurality of relations and identities* (Swamy 2016: 193). In South Asia a large number of people live in poverty and are exposed to various kinds of miseries. On the other hand, there are serious concerns of radicalisation and fundamentalism leading to communal violence. In this context, dialogue should not be confused with an attempt to unify all religions; it is a far more practical search. It is a search to recognise the identities and differences of others. It seeks to make space for others and leads us to justice. The reality that impacts dialogue is of the vast sections of society that are subject to different forms of injustices in all spheres of life. From the perspective of the margins, dialogue should be located within the plurality of liberative praxis among religions.

Dialogue: Plurality of Liberative Praxis

We believe it is unbiblical and unchristian to hold that divine liberative presence is confined to one religion, in this case Christianity. As pointed out in previous chapters, Jesus the Christ is not limited to one religious community. All religions contribute towards the unravelling of the divine, yet the divine remains a mystery. To believe in the life-giving creative power of God, to affirm the unbounded universality of divine grace and to profess the ever-forgiving abundance of divine mercy is to recognise and celebrate the dynamic and distinctive modes of the divine being and becoming among people of all faiths. All religions have an element of liberation; however, co-opted by the dominant sections of society, religions are also oppressive. A dialogical approach will exercise critical scrutiny of the history of every faith, recognising both the positive contribution to people's struggle for human dignity and the negative roles to legitimise unjust status quo. In every religion, it is possible to identify movements that have supported and revolted against injustice and oppression. The Bhakti movement in Hinduism challenged the discriminatory caste system. Religions like Buddhism and Sikhism were movements that came out against caste oppression strongly. But, as Sreenivasa Rao says, "There are also many negative examples such as the use of Christianity to legitimize feudalism, capitalism, racial discrimination, and sexism or the use of Hinduism to perpetuate the practice of caste discrimination and untouchability" (Sreenivasa 1991:166).

In dialogue, Christians actively respond to the command to 'love God and your neighbour as yourself'; it testifies the love experienced in Christ. So, the mission of the church in a pluralistic world is to participate in God's continuing mission in the world, together with our neighbours of other faiths. God in Jesus Christ himself has entered into a relationship with people of all faiths, offering the good news of salvation (Samartha 1981: 11). Moreover, there is a promise of Jesus Christ that the Holy Spirit will lead us into all truth; therefore, dialogue becomes the quest for truth because biblically truth cannot be realised in isolation (Samartha 1981: 11). The life and witness of the church in a religiously pluralistic context can only be successful if we are ready to share, in the life of the community, through partnership with the people of other faiths and ideologies, in the task of liberation.

Dialogue is an ethical imperative. "Dialogue is not a concept; it is a relationship; it is people sharing the meaning and mysteries of human existence, struggling together in suffering, hope and joy" (Winslow 1999: 18). In a pluralistic context we are not only called to be the witness of Jesus Christ and to his good news but are also challenged to get into dialogue with other living faiths and ideologies and see how God is active in the world.

Through IRD, Christian mission has a specific contribution to make in the life of the larger community. Dialogue enables Christians to join hands with the people of other faiths in an act of courage and sacrifice. Dialogue calls for common humanity to be sought in the midst of tensions in order to achieve social and structural renewal.

Religions have a dismal record in the history of community relations. Religions should be watchful of past mistakes, be humble in their claims and more realistic in offering solutions to political and social problems of the country (Samartha 1981: 124). The thrust and focus of dialogical praxis in South Asia should take into account the social condition of the land. Social conditions are represented by divisions on the basis of caste, class, religion, ethnicity and gender. For instance, the poor in South Asia face limitless oppression and are caught in a cycle of never-ending poverty. These oppressions are trans-religious and transcultural (Thumma 2000: 117). Everyone has the right to live, and dialogue should lead us to realise that the right to live is common to all human beings. Every religious community is confronted with a challenge to immerse itself into issues of poverty and plurality through dialogical and liberative activity. Therefore, a liberative praxis in dialogue is essential in the South Asian context. Developing on liberating praxis, our next section will focus on ethical norms for IRD.

Listening to Silenced Voices in Dialogue

In the first chapter we saw how Christianity appropriated dominant religious and cultural traditions in the process of being indigenous. We also observed that dialogue should not just remain an intellectual pursuit, focusing on understanding the dogmas and doctrines of other religions, but it should focus on contextual realities that affect the life of the people. In order to keep dialogue rooted in praxis, we need to hear voices that are not sufficiently represented in dialogue. Any discussion on these issues has to take into account the following.

Option for the Poor

Plurality and poverty are two important characteristics of Asian societies. Liberation of the people at the margins depends upon how pluralism is practised. The church is still located in the theology of missionaries and thereby unconsciously sides with oppressive ideologies. It is still located in numerical strength and aggressive evangelism. Hence, a perspective from the poor is integral for the church to be an event. Pluralism affirms the need to uphold the cause of the poor and the marginalised. Thus justice, peace and freedom are integral towards the theology of interreligious engagements. IRD has to begin with the option for the poor. There has to be a collaborative effort to understand the language of victims and victimisation. The church has to engage itself in liberation because of its commitment to Jesus and faith in Christ. Brazilian theologian Leonardo Boff, who is known for his active support of liberation theology, points out that,

> Option for the poor occupy epistemological locus; that is, the poor constitute the point from which one attempts to conceive of God, Christ, grace, history, the mission of Churches, the meaning of economy, politics and the future of societies and human beings. From that standpoint we realise to what extent the present societies are exclusionary, to what extent democracies are imperfect, to what extent religions and churches are tied to the interest of the powerful (Boff 1997: 107).

Jesus was disturbed by poverty and injustice in his environment (Koch 1999: 99-100). Therefore, he proclaimed God's solidarity with all those who were victims of systemic injustice. The historical Jesus operated in a world where poverty was considered a sin and punishment from God. In that world he sided with the poor, countering the theology of the oppressors and developing a programme to strengthen and liberate the oppressed. The poor remind the church that love means to recreate, to make new the situation of human beings by taking into account the concrete causes of dehumanisation (Sobrino 1985: 7). According to Bryant L. Myers, the church should become a hermeneutical community that relates the biblical world concretely to the circumstances of its time, place and culture (Myers 1999: 127-128). The poor give love its urgency and the poor give a concrete name to sin (Sobrino 1985: 108). Option for the poor can become an effective ground on which Christians can deliberate and collaborate with other religions of this world.

However, this is not to say that only the poor need liberation. Liberation is an all-inclusive reality; the poor needs liberation from the exploitation by the rich and the rich needs liberation from their selfish attitude. Option for the poor brings a sense of perspective towards liberation and the establishment of a just society. It is an inclusive approach that directs us to genuinely marginalised groups. The point is not just speaking for the poor but realising that they are agents of their own history and liberation. Option for the poor also makes us aware of the fact that the poor in their own creative way resist oppression, and IRD can be a platform through which the church understands such resistances effectively and does not make the mistake of imposing its own agenda. Option for the poor gets liberation praxis rooted in the socio-cultural-economic truths of the marginal communities in South Asia. It challenges all religions to understand and partner each other and commit themselves to the task of liberation. In the South Asian context, salvation can be best described as liberation.

Option for Indigenous People: Creation Perspective

Anthropocentrism has been a dominant theme in missionary theology and later theological development. Western anthropocentrism saw God in terms of the image of human beings. However, an anthropocentric understanding has no real concern for the preservation and protection of earth (John 2012: 45). Western churches, particularly since the Reformation, have been almost anthropocentric in their teaching and have had no regard for the non-human elements in God's creation (Bradley 1990: 2). So, they tended to overlook the spirituality rooted in creation and the perspective of indigenous communities. Failing to notice the creation aspect resulted in the alienation of indigenous people. Wati Longchar points out that,

> One feels that unless the perspective of creation spirituality on indigenous people is made central to the process of interfaith dialogue, indigenous people and the other marginalized groups like tribals, dalits and women who live and work close to the soil will always be looked down upon as inferior socially, culturally and even spiritually (Longchar 2002: 71).

Since South Asia has a large population of indigenous people, their worldview needs to be properly represented in IRD. Indigenous worldviews/visions are dependent upon the land/forest and the place they live in. The indigenous people consider land as a gift from God and that they are not owners but custodians of it. It is land that gives them identity and security. Nirmal Minz, an authority on tribal and indigenous people and culture, points out that indigenous history is rooted in land, and land is key to their identity as people; tribal identity cannot be imagined without land (Minz 1994: 13). Wati Longchar defines the importance of the land thus,

> For Tribal, Land is life. The land is the source of our origin, our nourishment, our support and identity. The land is not mere

> space; it is a place and a symbol of unity which gives identity
> to the community. The land owns the people. If there is no
> land, there is no community, personhood and identity.... In a
> tribal world view, a human has no moral right to treat the land
> as a mere object to be used and exploited (Longchar 1998:73).

Land is so sacred for indigenous people that their very life and livelihood is integrated with the land (Ralte 2005: 34). Even tribal consciousness is related to land. Minz opines that the corporate and the communitarian identity of the indigenous, including their land and forest, is characteristic of their consciousness (Minz 1989: 20). But Christian theology and methodology of IRD has neglected this significance for land; the dominant Christian tradition has only focused on humans as the central point of creation.

The issue of land/space highlights a few important methodological considerations that have remained silent in IRD. First, theology from the indigenous perspective seeks to look at space considering the fact that life cannot be conceived without creation. Space is the point of reference and the key to understanding human selfhood, God and spirit. Second, it makes the world aware of the interrelatedness of indigenous life with land. Third, when our theological endeavours seek liberation from the land perspective, human life would be automatically inculcated in the whole programme of liberation. Fourth, space becomes the foundation of liberation. The fifth and the most significant aspect is that the land perspective creates an opportunity to reconsider and re-evaluate traditional views on God, Spirit and salvation, including human beings' place in creation (Vashum 2007:25).

The root cause of major interreligious conflicts has been our exploitative attitude towards creation. Theology from the perspective of the indigenous people provides ground for peaceful and just coexistence of not only all religions but also of human beings with creation. The stress is on the interconnectedness and interdependence of all created order. Relationship with the earth is 'part of the being' of all created beings. Thus, in nature, everything affects everything else (Nalunnakkal 1999: 225). This implies that the earth is the common mother of both animals and humans. The disregard to interconnectedness has had devastating effects on ecology. This approach will help us in realising that human beings are just one part of many in nature.

Option for Women

Feminist theologians argue that the dialogue programme has suffered from the insufficient involvement of women and the absence of women's concerns in the issues taken up for dialogue. Women have actively participated in dialogue, but the overall picture remains poor. Sexism that pervades in religious traditions affects dialogue too. The participation of women is only symbolic than real as men set both the agenda and the framework of discussion. Ursula King says it is evident that interreligious dialogue remains part of patriarchy (cited in Ariarajah 1999: 60-61). She says "to envision the development of post-patriarchal dialogue, it will be necessary to do away with the hierarchies of gender which is persuasive in religion. Radical institution and doctrinal transformation are needed to respond to the needs of women for equal participation and dignity, and the demand to condemn all prejudice and violence against women, especially those done in the name of religion" (Cited in Ariarajah 1999: 60-61).

The implication of IRD for women is threefold (O'Neill 1990: 102-104). Firstly, women will have greater awareness and appreciation of diversity among themselves. Through this an atmosphere of trust will be created and diverse perspectives clarified. Secondly, there will arise a need for women to reflect on and write about their conversations. Interreligious dialogue must forsake preconceived notions and place concepts such as liberation, oppression and feminism (which cannot be assumed) specifically in the context of social change and thus prevent relevant theorising. Thirdly, women will be more prepared to act for social change. Dialogue is a commitment; only through dialogue will women come to learn each other's needs, the extent of oppression and find the most effective way to end them. Through dialogue and literature, women will be able to share their experiences with each other. Such communication will empower women involved in interreligious dialogue to act more dynamically.

Mission of the Church

We believe it is unbiblical to be exclusive. The exclusive character of the church should give away to a more inclusive approach. The mission of the church should no more be triumphalistic, focusing on increase in the number of members. It has to adopt a more inclusive approach where ideas of partnership, togetherness, relationships, mutual recognition and respect define the church's attitude towards other religions. This section seeks to investigate an approach that fosters inclusivity.

Justice and Inclusivity of the Kingdom of God

German Lutheran theologian Wolfhart Pannenberg points out that everything in Jesus's message is dominated by the idea of the immanent kingdom of God (Pannenberg 1977: 54). It forms the heart of Jesus's message to humanity. Jesus's message of the kingdom reflects both future and present dimensions. John

Sobrino says the attempt to approach the historical Jesus must be done from the standpoint of the kingdom of God (Sobrino, 1978:60). Kingdom suggests the totality of Jesus's action for the renewal of this world. It was the vulnerable, the poor and the oppressed that found place in the kingdom. This suggests that the kingdom of God includes social witness. The liberation of the oppressed from exploitation and monopoly capitalism, caste structure, and political and priestly domination is necessary for Christian social witness (Thomas 2007: 39). Therefore, the kingdom becomes a present reality and has its practical implications for our life on earth. The blessed in the kingdom are those who identify themselves with the dispossessed in society and extend them the right hand of fellowship, and those who seek to create a social order that will respect the humanity of the downtrodden (Thomas 2007: 99). Therefore, love is the basic principle of the kingdom which results in justice. The kingdom is not a territory but an order; it is a revolution in thinking and action. The kingdom becomes the effective word of Jesus, and his teachings spell out ethical radicalism.

The kingdom of God belongs to all, irrespective of one's social location or religious standing. The decision to be a part of it depends upon us. The entire mission of Jesus was determined by his message of God's sovereign rule (Jonge 1992: 10). He pointed out that the reign of God was made up of outcasts and strangers (Song 1993: 43). Historically, this would have been such a radical message because all those who were considered to be unrighteous, unholy, were to be a part of it. It not only brought every human being to the same level but considered all humanity as equal in front of God. As Choan-Seng Song says, the Christian church that is not able to envision with Jesus this vision of God's reign cannot preach Jesus (Song 1993: 26).

For the church, the kingdom of God should become a message that entails hope for liberation. It should be seen as liberating from legalism, authoritarianism and forces that dominate and oppress. The message of the kingdom unveils the vision of a new polity in which life with dignity, justice and opportunities are available for all. The church is not a hierarchical structure or an embodiment of unjust values with vested interests. Rather, it is a visible sign of God's kingdom which fosters equality and justice. Through the message of the kingdom, Jesus points out that God's face is the face of outcasts (Song 1993: 45).

But the fact is that a number of issues in South Asia perpetuate injustice and violence. The church ceases to be liberative if it cannot join hands with other religions for the establishment of a world where liberation is a lived experience. The kingdom of God becomes a realised eschatology, a future reality, when liberation is realised in the present through collaborative human action.

Recognising Spirit outside the Church

Modern theology protects itself of Christomonism (accepting one divine person, Jesus Christ, rather than the Trinity) and adopts a Trinitarian framework. It has come to recognise the fact that Jesus has to be located in the framework of the Trinity. This framework is referred to as pneumatology (the branch of Christian theology concerned with the Holy Spirit). It aims at interpreting the universal dimension of the Christ event, in recognition of the Holy Spirit in Christian communities, as the spirit of the Son (SVD 2005: 258). Pneumatology brings into dialogue the Spirit in history, the work of the Spirit in the present and the future, and the universal salvific will of God.

Marcus J. Borg points out that the pre-Easter Jesus was a 'spirit person.' He uses 'spirit' as a synonym for God. A spirit person is a person to whom the sacred is an experiential reality. Such persons experience the sacred more frequently through the realities of life. Thereby, they are best known cross-culturally. They become the mediators of the sacred and the funnels for the power or wisdom of God to enter this world. They connect their community with spirit. In this sense, Jesus was a spirit person (Borg 1994: 31-36).

The experience of the Spirit in Jesus's life was not individualistic; it was corporate and was integral to his mission. The presence of this corporate aspect of the Spirit in Jesus makes him a social person (Moltmann 1990:1). Jesus was thus a social prophet who challenged social boundaries defined by the elite with an alternative social vision (Borg 1997: 1). Therefore, praxis is integral to the works of the Spirit. Service to humanity and liberation of the oppressed best express the works of the Holy Spirit in the world today. Samuel Rayan strengthens this by asserting that Jesus becomes the symbol of the Holy Spirit (Rayan 2003:79). Pneumatology affirms that the Spirit of God is operative in all religions.

Through IRD the work of the Spirit should be characterised by an attitude of cooperation with the wider liberation movement and of witness of the work of the Spirit outside the church. Spiritual movements outside the church can be reflected in other religions' local culture, art forms, dances, musical performances and everything that entails in itself the possibility of a better future and resistance against oppression. This will help us realise that theology is a reflection of the culture in which a religion operates.

This will help us recognise and observe the fact that God communicates with all creation equally, through diverse modes and methods. We become aware of the fact that God is working through all religions for the renewal of society. Ideological and physical communion with Spirit movements outside of the church would only enrich the church. The Spirit cannot be bound, limited and restricted.

To work for the oppressed in spiritual cooperation, there is a need to move beyond personal satisfaction and holiness resulting from the Spirit to communal and cooperative elements that the Sprit entails. Our quest to do so helps us in transcending the walls of the church. The liberation movement thus becomes all-encompassing and all-inclusive.

Church as an Open Liberative Space

The church has to deal with alternative/multiple spaces for emancipation in a positive way. IRD should help the church to become an open liberative space. This openness can challenge fundamentalism in the present context. In their quest for emancipation, converts from among the marginalised groups have seen the church as a place they belong to. As seen in first chapter, Dalits saw the church as a space that would enable them to break away from the structure of caste. The church as an emancipatory space has significant implications for them. The marginalised saw the church as a space that could offer liberation and healing from violence, oppression and humiliation. But Dalits were discriminated in the church too, both at the altar and in the pews. They were pushed out from this holy space.

Historically, we see Jesus violating spaces that were considered to be holy. Inspired by Jesus, the church should become an ideological space and ground for better involvement with other religious traditions. In partnership, it should violate spaces that promote discrimination. In a situation where the space for the marginalised is shrunk, the church can provide them an *'open space'* for planning and implementing emancipatory agendas. It should become an open space which produces fruits of justice, peace and equality. IRD offers the church an opportunity to become this open liberative space.

Church as an Agent of Alternative Memory

The politics of memory lies at the heart of liberation. Alternative memories enable a process of remembering the past in order to look towards a future of hope. The stories the marginalised narrate, form an alternative memory, which enables them to become subjects in their own historical events. IRD presents an opportunity for the marginalised to come together and share their stories of marginalisation and resistance. This helps them articulate and possess their historical consciousness. The church can thus become an agent that initiates and fosters alternative memory.

In partnership with other religions and the marginalised, the church should start a process to write themselves into salvation history. Creation stories, songs of indigenous people, stories of oppression of women and other marginal groups can become resources for theologising. C.S Song points out that many biblical scholars and theologians take it for granted that Christian faith and theology are *sui generis,* normative for cultures outside Christianity (Song 2011: 16). It is typical for the subjects of all other cultures and religions to be subjected to scrutiny, criticism, even rejection (Song 2011: 16). Such attitudes were evident in in missionary theology.

Life realities and stories of the marginalised should become archetypes in themselves. According to Kosuke Koyama, when theological methodology takes into consideration local sources, it becomes a lived methodology (Koyama 1999: X). For the church to become a living one, it should be located in places of local power (life realities). Through participation with other religions, recovering and narrating stories from the underside, the church can become an agent of creative encounter between the experience of God, the world, and human beings in their concrete world realities.

Church as a Social Movement

The discussion in this chapter points out that the church has to become a social movement (Longchar: 2008: 39) that encounters and confronts oppressive structures, and discriminative ideologies and attitudes. This has to be done with a vision of dismantling everything that instigates and promotes oppression and discrimination. It has to give up its institutional character and work to reform the community from below (Moltmann 1997: 329). It has to get involved and understand resistive strategies of communities at the grassroots level. Therefore, Azariah's contention that local churches should make use of social analysis for their mission and ministry is of extreme importance (Azariah 2000: 106). Social analysis makes us aware that in order to make our approachs more inclusive, it has to begin from below (Dietrich & Wielenga 2011: 27).

Jesus was sensitive to the social location and status of the oppressed in his world. He named them, recognised their identities and then worked for their renewal. Similarly, the church has to demonstrate seriousness and commitment to social causes, not in isolation but in partnership with other religious traditions and movements. It has to resist the dominant culture. The church should become an active part of the liberation movement and express its solidarity with the oppressed community. Grassroots communities are 'prophetic leaven' for the renewal of the church and society (Moltmann 1977: 330) Therefore, the church should cater to the needs and aspirations of the oppressed and at the same time be impacted upon by them. This would protect the church from imposing the mission of liberation on the marginalised. Being impacted upon would mean that the church would identify itself with the marginalised and participate in their struggle for justice and liberation along with other religious traditions.

Conclusion

For any kind of dialogue, it is important to begin with a commitment to the weaker sections of society. Dialogue as empowerment has a great significance in the South Asian context. It is evident from our above discussions that interreligious dialogue is not different from mission. In the present context it should become the mission of the church. Missionary theology only focused on preaching. IRD corrects this approach and makes praxis its mission strategy. Dialogue is very much the part of mission and holds a great responsibility for Christians in the modern world, which is rapidly undergoing changes.

A Christian dialogue implies neither the denial of uniqueness of Christ nor any loss of commitment to Christ, but rather a genuine Christian approach which should be human, personal, relevant and humble. It is a part of a living relationship between people of different faiths, identities and ideologies as they share in the life of a community. While affirming the lordship of Jesus Christ, IRD helps us to recognise the people of other faiths as our fellow pilgrims. Dialogue is not an alternative to mission, but it is a plan to build and plant a new concept of witness, and the new principle of the involvement of the church in social realms in partnership with other religions.

Bibliography

Ariarajah, Wesley. "The Understanding of Practice of Dialogue: Its Nature, Purpose and Variation." In *Faiths in the Midst of Faiths, Reflections on Dialogue in Community* edited by S. J. Samartha Geneva: WCC, 1977.

Ariarajah, Wesley. *Not Without My Neighbour: Issues In interfaith Dialogue.* Switzerland: WCC Publication, 1999.

Azariah, M. *A Pastor's Search for Dalit Theology.* New Delhi: ISPCK, 2000.

Boff, Leonardo *Cry of The Earth, Cry of The Poor.* Maryknoll, NY: Orbis Books, 1997.

Borg, Marcus J. "From Galilean Jew To The Face of God: The Pre-Easter and Post-Easter Jesus." In *Jesus at 2000.* Edited by Marcus J. Borg USA: Westview Press, 1997.

Borg, Marcus J. *Meeting Jesus Again for the First Time: The Historical Jesus & The Heart of Contemporary Faith.* San Francisco: Harper & Collins, 1994.

Bradley, Ian. *God is Green.* London: Dartorn, Longman and Todd, 1990.

Bryant L. Myers, *Walking with the Poor: Principles and Practice of Transformational Development.* (Maryknoll/New York: Orbis Books/ World Vision, 1999), 127-128.

C.S. Song, "Doing Theology with Stories: Theological Education, Where Do We Go From Here," *The Journal For Theologies and Culture In Asia* Vol. 10 (2011): 16.

Dietrich Gabriela & Bas Wielenga, *Towards Understanding Indian Society.* Tiruvalla: Christava Sahitya Samithi, 2011.

Hallencreutz, Carl F. *Dialogue and Community: Ecumenical Issues in Inter-Religious Relationships.* Geneva: WCC, 1977.

John, V J. "Biblical and Theological Legitimacy on Theologies of Ecology." *The Journal of Theologies and Cultures in Asia Vol 11* (2012), 44-57.

Jonge, Marinus de. "The Christological Significance of Jesus' Preaching of the Kingdom of God." In *The Future of Christology: Essays in Honor of Leander E. Keck.* Edited by Abraham J. Malherbe and Wayne A. Meeks. Minneapolis: Fortress Press, 1993.

Kinnamon Michael & Brian E. Cope, *The Ecumenical Movement.* Michigan: Edermans Pub. Co., 1997

Koch, Klaus. *From Amos to Jesus: Biblical Eschatology and Its Social Implications.* Bangalore: UTC, 1999.

Koyama, Kosuke. *Water Buffalo Theology*, 25th Anniversary Edition. New York: Orbis Books, 1999.

Lee, Minkyu. *The Breaking of Bread and the Breaking of Boundaries: A Study of the Metaphor of Bread in the Gospel of Matthew.* New York: Peter Lang, 2015.

Longchar, Wati. "A Critique on Christian theology of Creation." In *Doing Theology with Tribal Resources: Context and Perspective.* Edited by Wati Longchar and Larry E. Davis. Jorhat: Tribal Study Center, 1998.

Longchar, Wati. "Inter-Religious Theological Methodology from The Location of Indigenous People In Asia." In *Inter-Cultural Asian Theological Methodologies: An Exploration.* Edited by Samson Prabhakar. Bangalore: SATHRI, 2002.

Longchar, Wati. "The continuity of Indigenous People in Today's World." In *Garnering Tribal Resources for Doing Tribal Christian Theology.* Edited by Razouselie Lasetso. Jorhat: ETC, 2008.

McGrath, Alister E. *An Introduction Christian Theology: 3rd Ed.* USA: Blackwell Publishers, 2001.

Minz, Nirmal. "In Search of Roots: A Tribal Perspective." *Religion and Society* 41/1 (March 1994): 21-25.

Minz, Nirmal. "Meaning of Tribal Consciousness." *Religion and Society* 36/2 (June 1989): 12-23.

Minz, Nirmal. "Tribal Perspective on Ecology." In *the Tribal World View on Ecology.* Tribal Study Series No. 2. Edited by Wati Longchar and Yangkahao Vashum. Jorhat: Tribal Study Center, 1998.

Moltmann, Jürgen. *Church in The Power of the Spirit,* translated by Margaret Kohl. London: SCM Press, 1977.

Moltmann, Jürgen. *The Way of Jesus Christ: Christology in Messianic Dimensions,* translated by Margaret Kohl. London: SCM Press, 1990.

Nalunnakkal, George Mathew. *Green Liberation: Towards an Integral Ecotheology.* Delhi: ISPCK/NCCI, 1999.

O'Neill, Maura *Women Speaking, Women Listening: Women In Inter Religious Dialogue.* Maryknoll: Orbis Books, 1990.

Pannenberg, Wolfhart. *The Theology of The Kingdom of God*, Richard John Neuhaus. Ed. Philadelphia: The West Minister Press, 1977.

Pui-lan, Kwok. "Ecology and Recycling of Christianity." In *Ecotheology: Voices from the South and North*. Edited by David G. Hallman. New York/Switzerland: WCC/Orbis Books, 1994.

Ralte, Lalrinawmi. "Issue of Identity: A Tribal Women Perspective." *Religion and Society 50/3* (September, 2005): 25-35.

Rao, Sreenivasa. *Inter-faith Dialogue and World Community*. Madras: The Christian Literature Society, 1991.

Rayan, Samuel "Symbols of the Spirit," *Ministerial Formation 50* (July, 1990): 9-10. Cited by, Kirsten Kim, *Mission in The Spirit: The Holy Spirit In Indian Christian Theologies*. Delhi: ISPCK, 2003.

Samartha S.J. *Courage for Dialogue: Ecumenical Issues in Inter-Religious Relationship*. Geneva: WCC, 1981.

Selvanayagam, Israel. *A Dialogue on Dialogue*. Madras: Christian literature Society, 1995.

Sobrino, Jon. *The True Church and Poor*. London: SCM Press, 1985.

Sobrino,Jon. *Christology at the Cross Roads: A Latin American Approach*. London: SCM Press Ltd., 1978.

Song, C. S. *Jesus and The Reign of God*. Minneapolis: Fortress Press, 1993.

SVD, Mohan Doss. *Christ in Spirit*. Delhi: ISPCK, 2005.

Thomas, M. M. *In Jesus The Kingdom of God is Near: Luke 9-19*. Translated by. T. M. Philip. Tiruvalla: CSS books & BTTBPSA, 2007.

Thumma, Anthoniraj. *Breaking Barriers: Liberation of Dialogue and Dialogue of Liberation*. Delhi: ISPCK 2000.

Vashum, Yangkahao. "Indigenous Theology as Postcolonial Theology: A Methodological Consideration." In *Tribal Christian Theology: Methods and Sources For Constructing a Relevant Theology for the Indigenous People of North East*. Tribal Study Series No. 15. Edited by Razouselie Lasetse and Yangkhao Vashum. Jorhat: Eastern Theological College, 2007.

Winslow, D. John. *Dialogue in a Religiously Pluralistic Context*. Trivandrum: Bright Printers, 1999.

Building Interfaith Solidarities for Justice

Text: Isaiah 44: 28–45: 5

One of the major themes in the Bible is the liberation of the poor and the oppressed. Both in the Old Testament (also called the Hebrew Bible) as well as the New Testament, there is a recurring emphasis on God's preferential option for the poor and the marginalised. This accentuation on justice has been at the root of social gospel, liberation theology and hermeneutics, and the socio-political engagement of the church in general. However, in this work for justice and peace, what is the role of other religious faiths and communities? The text from Isaiah could throw some light on this question.

Text in its Context

This prophecy is set in the context of the exile of the people of Judah. Though it was quite different from the slavery of their ancestors in Egypt many centuries ago, it was still a humiliating and shameful experience for them. After all, Jerusalem was captured and their temple destroyed. It was only natural for such people to expect a leader, perhaps someone like Moses, to liberate them and lead them back to their homeland.

However, this time the new liberator comes from outside. It is Cyrus, the Persian emperor. It is he, according to the Lord, who is the shepherd (generally used to refer to Israelite kings and priests) and the one who will carry out the divine purpose. He is the Lord's anointed one, the messiah, a term that will gain more significance in later centuries and especially in the Christian discourse. However, here, in this point in history, it is a 'heathen' king who is the messiah. And God does what he always does for his chosen leaders: subdue nations before him, open doors before him, go before him and level the mountains, and give him treasures of darkness and riches (Isaiah 45: 1–3). All this is done so that Cyrus may know that it is the Lord who calls him, even though he did not worship the God of Israel.

The author, the prophet Isaiah, seems to make some definite assertions here. First, he is confident that the Lord wants to free and restore the people of Judah. This is almost a repeat of the great Exodus experience. The people of Israel are in a foreign land under the rule of a foreign king. They are eager to return home to freedom, and God hears their cries. It is well in line with the pattern of divine intervention for liberation of the subjugated people.

Second, Isaiah believes that Cyrus is the hero of this story. And it is none other than the Lord who has chosen Cyrus. God is responsible for the success of Cyrus, even if Cyrus is not aware of it. This means that God has deliberately chosen a foreign king to enact his justice.

What can be inferred from this is that the God of Israel is not reluctant to bring outsiders, people of other faiths, to enact justice and liberate the exiles. In this story of the "new exodus," people are reminded that divine justice is not limited to or by religious boundaries. It is no more 'us versus them.' The work for justice is not exclusively Christian. Other faith communities rooted in their own faiths are an essential part in the work of liberation and emancipation of those who are victims of unjust structural suffering.

A question might arise in our minds: what about the condemnation of idols and other gods that we often read about in the Bible, especially in the prophetic literature? While this can be a prolonged discussion, let us only consider the basic things. First, we must recall from chapter 2 that religion until the modern period was always deeply political. Allegiance to a particular deity was related to a person's communal identity. The condemnation of other gods meant condemnation of gods of other nations, often enemy nations. This strong sentiment based on one's devotion towards one's nation and deity involved an attitude of "whose god is better, and my god is the strongest."

Second, in the Bible, idols and other gods are often related to oppression and injustice. For instance, in the Exodus story, the gods of Egypt are not simply foreign gods but also deities who were responsible for the oppression of the Israelites. These gods, represented in human form by the pharaohs, were responsible for the enslavement of the Israelites whereas Yahweh stood for the liberation of the enslaved and exploited people. It was a battle of the gods for justice.

Above all, we saw in chapter 4 that monotheism is the basic tenet of the Israelite religion and Judaism. God is one. Of that there is no doubt. This is the commandment. And, from their own perspective, for the prophets of Israel, Yahweh was that one God. He demanded loyalty from his chosen people, but other people who were not part of this covenant were free to worship whichever deity they wanted, even if, from the point of view of Israel, these 'religious others' were also under the power of the one God. It is the same God who is present to everyone even while giving them the freedom to worship whom and how they please. The only criterion seems to be the question of justice. When anyone is oppressed and treated unjustly, Yahweh takes offence against the people and the deities who perpetuate this injustice.

On the other hand, from this prophecy of Isaiah, we see that commitment to justice can bring people of different faiths together. In a sense, we can say that there is an inclusivistic (or pluralistic, depending on how we view this) outlook here: everyone worships God in their own way and they can all come together to work for the liberation of the oppressed (see chapter 3).

Text in our Context

In recent times, theologians like Paul Knitter have emphasised precisely this biblical truth. They argue that justice can and should be the centre and goal of dialogue and interreligious engagement, especially from a Christian point of view. In many ways, every religion, in its own distinct way, foregrounds the well-being of humanity and all creation. And, all religions, including Christianity, have their blind spots, their limitations, and dark side. We know only too well the destruction Christians, including missionaries, wrought in many parts of the world in the name of evangelism. Without denying the good that Christianity has done, we should also acknowledge that Christianity—or rather the (mis)interpretation of the Christian gospel—is guilty of slavery, colonialism, annihilation of cultures, holocaust, to name a few. This is also true of other religions. All religions have their good, life-affirming aspects, as well as bad, life-denying elements.

This is why it is necessary for religions and religious communities to engage in dialogue and collaboration. There is much that other faiths have to offer from their wealth of wisdom to enhance and enrich, and—respectfully and cautiously—challenge and critique one another. From a Christian point of view, this text on the calling of Cyrus, the gentile, underscores the value of other faiths and faith communities in the struggle for liberation of the marginalised. It invites the church to include and involve other religious communities and their beliefs and practices in the ongoing work of justice. After all, to recall the words of Abraham Joshua Heschel, the Jewish philosopher-activist who stood and fought along with Rev. Dr. Martin Luther King Jr., "no religion is an island" (Heschel 1966: 1).

To ponder and discuss:

1. *Did Cyrus really know the God of Israel? Did he ever acknowledge it?*

2. *Did Cyrus become a follower of Yahweh?*

3. *What religious aspects of his religious beliefs did Cyrus bring to the table?*

4. *What can other faith communities through their faith contribute towards justice in your local community?*

Bibliography

Heschel, Abraham Joshua. "No religion is an Island" *Union Seminary Quarterly Review* XXI/2, Part 2. January 1966: 117–134.

Banquet Beyond Boundaries:
A Re-vision of the Kingdom of Heaven

Text: Matthew 8: 5–13

The story of the healing of the servant of the Roman centurion is popular among Christians as an example of faith. But what more does this story of a *gentile* centurion teach us?

Text in its Context

The healing of the centurion's servant forms a part of a larger block of healing stories. Following the famous Sermon on the Mount (chapters 5–7), and the healing of the person with a skin disease, someone generally treated as an outcast, Matthew writes about the healing of another outsider. As Anna Case-Winters notes,

> The healing stories … show Jesus interacting with and healing a number of people who, for one reason or another, live at the margins of community and cultic life or are even excluded from these circles: a leper, a centurion (not only a Gentile, but a representative of Roman oppression), a servant, persons possessed by demons, a little girl, and a woman with a flow of blood (unclean). The overlooked and the excluded are included in his ministry of healing. (Case-Winters 2015: 126–127)

It is also quite clear that the evangelist was trying to show, through these stories placed adjacent to each other, the universal lordship of Jesus over all people, irrespective of who they were. This is evident through the humble words of the centurion: "I am not worthy…." But, as important as Jesus is to this story, we cannot ignore the Roman centurion who earned Jesus's praise.

As is the case with many other healing stories, we do not know too many details about the centurion. But based on the gospels, we get the following picture. He was surely one of the several centurions posted in Palestine. And, from the words of Jesus we can infer that he was definitely not Jewish. However, in his version of the story, Luke notes that he was friends with the Jews and had even built them the synagogue in Capernaum (Luke 7: 1–10). It is also possible to say that though he knew about Jesus (through other Jews?), he was, most likely, not a follower of Jesus. Both Matthean and Lucan narratives indicate this was the (gentile Roman) centurion's first encounter with Jesus.

This could explain Jesus's response to the centurion. Though according to the English translation (NRSV) Jesus's response to the centurion was positive—"I will go and cure him"—the Greek suggests a more hesitant response: "Am I to go and heal him?" It is suggested that this makes more sense given Jesus's reluctance to heal gentiles (cf. the healing of the daughter of the Canaanite woman in Matthew 15: 21–31) (Case-Winters 2015: 128). But the centurion seems to relieve Jesus of the predicament and expresses his faith in Jesus's ability to heal from a distance.

In spite of his reluctance, after listening to the centurion, Jesus changes his mind. He goes on to make two statements that demonstrate his changed attitude towards the religious 'other.' First, by commending the faith of the centurion, Jesus shows that faith in God is not limited to any particular religious group. In fact, as Jesus notes, the centurion's faith is more than the faith of his own people. A heathen, a religious outsider, becomes the example of faith for none other than God's own chosen people. Jesus's assertion challenges those who claim to be 'insiders' and believe that they are closer to and know God. This critique of the insiders becomes even clearer when we remember that this healing story follows the Sermon on the Mount in which Jesus portrays himself as the new Moses, the new prophet of Israel who leads his people into greater depths of faith. Through his religious neighbour, Jesus reminds his followers (and his fellow religious members) that God is not held captive by human(-constructed) boundaries.

In his second statement Jesus goes a bit further. He declares that it is people like the centurion who will come and join the banquet with the great patriarchs in the kingdom of heaven. The banquet is an important theme in Israelite/Jewish worldview (Isaiah 2: 2-4, 25: 6; 43: 5-6) which stresses the special communion/relationship that they will have with God. Though the texts in Isaiah do not necessarily refer to the kingdom of heaven, Jesus uses the image to illustrate the point that God's community is not limited to any particular group of people. The phrase "many will come from the east and the west" signifies that the whole human community is invited to and will be present at the banquet.

This is followed by a polemical declaration by Jesus that the "heirs of the kingdom" will be thrown into the outer darkness…." We should be careful not to jump into anti-Jewish/anti-Semitic interpretations and judge the faith of the Jewish people or suggest that they will be thrown in hell. That certainly is not the point here. Rather, Jesus's words emphasise the faith that a person from a different religious community had in Jesus as a man of God, and spirit of humility. It also shows that those who claim to know God and boast of a special relationship with God need to be careful. Those who are heirs *could* be rejected and punished, while those who are considered—and often looked down upon—as outsiders will be invited and honoured. Simply put: The kingdom of heaven will have all sorts of people from various traditions who have faith in God!

Text in our Context

Most Christians believe in heaven. Though there is no one understanding of heaven in the scripture, many Christians imagine that heaven is a place exclusively meant for Christians— those who believe in Jesus Christ and are saved by him. The corollary of this view is that all ('others') who are not Christian (i.e. non-Christian) will go to hell, a place of damnation and eternal suffering. Such beliefs have not only led some people to disrespect other religions but also to condemn them as evil. This passage, however, seems to paint a different picture.

In this text, Jesus's understanding of heaven, or, to be precise, the kingdom of heaven, does not match with popular Christian notions. The kingdom of heaven is not a mono-religious gathering. It is not limited to people who profess a particular faith. It is not restricted to the followers of Jesus aka Christians. Rather, it is a multifaith community of love and fellowship. It is not simply heaven, but the kingdom of heaven, where God and God's values of justice and peace reign. To imagine and believe in a heaven that is only Christian is therefore against what Jesus taught. If God brings all her children together to the heavenly banquet, who are we to claim that heaven is only for Christians?

To ponder and discuss:

1. *How does this healing story relate to the Sermon on the Mount?*

2. *What do you think of the faith of the centurion?*

3. *Do you think the centurion became a follower of Jesus after this encounter?*

4. *Have you come across similar incidents in your own life?*

Bibliography

Case-Winters, Anna. Matthew. Westminster John Knox Press, 2015.

Jesus the Interreligious Learner

Text: Mark 7: 24–30

Among the many healing stories found in the Gospel, this is a rather unusual one. Also found in Matthew, this miracle paints a picture of Jesus that is not, at least explicitly, kind and gentle. Rather, he comes across as rude and crude in his language towards the woman who is identified as a Syrophoenician in the story. But even more interesting is to see Jesus, who not only 'tones down' his language and attitude and performs his healing, but also goes on, in Matthew's version of the story (Matthew 15: 21–28), to appreciate the faith of the 'gentile' woman. What does this passage teach us about religious diversity and learning from our religious neighbours?

Text in its Context

Mark notes that the story is set in the region of Tyre and Sidon (as found in some ancient authorities). Given their stereotypical negative popularity as heathen cities in the Old Testament prophetic literature, it is possible that Mark uses the names of these cities to "signify the whole Gentile world" (Lee 2015: 115). Therefore, Jesus going to the region of Tyre and Sidon marks an important phase in his ministry. He has clearly entered a gentile space. Of course, in ancient times, and more so in the context of the Roman Empire, borders could not be viewed as they are today, say between India and Pakistan. But, nonetheless, the mention of the two cities marks the religio-cultural differences between the two places and the people who inhabit them.

In any case, as we see, "he could not escape notice" (v. 24). A woman whose little daughter was possessed by an unclean spirit heard about him and found him. While Matthew notes that she was a Canaanite woman, Mark is a bit more specific and says that she was a gentile of Syrophoenician origin. The sentence is introduced with the conjunction 'now' to draw attention to her identity. Mark emphasises the fact that she was a gentile, a *hellenis* (which literally means Greek). But the use of the identifiers Canaanite and Syrophoenician seems to indicate that she was, in a sense, from an ancient gentile stock. She is the descendant of the old and stereotypical 'other' to the Israelites/Jews. If we take into account the mention of Tyre and Sidon, which represent the entire gentile world, this double emphasis on gentile and Syrophoenician identities of the woman could mean that the Gospel writer is using her to symbolise all gentiles. She represents all those who are (considered as) 'the other,' in particular, 'the religious other.'

The objective of the woman's visit is clear: to ask Jesus to heal her demon-possessed daughter. Mark writes that the woman 'begged' Jesus to indicate both her helplessness as well as Jesus's superior position in this story. Matthew sounds as if she found him on the road and followed him much to the (seeming) annoyance of his disciples. But Matthew also says that she used Jewish religio-cultural vocabulary to address him: "Have mercy on me, Lord, Son of David..." (Matthew 15: 22), indicating her familiarity with the Jewish worldview. Of course, this need not surprise us since, as mentioned earlier, borders were porous in the first century Roman Empire and it was quite possible that she was aware of, and even believed in, Jewish healers. Moreover, as Matthew was writing to a predominantly Jewish/Christian-Jewish audience, his way of narrating this story is understandable.

Nonetheless, the focus turns to Jesus's unusual response. While in general Jesus responds kindly and usually promptly to requests for healing and exorcism, in this case, he sounds rather unkind and indifferent, to put it mildly. In Mark, his answer is straightforward: "Let the children be fed first, for it is not fair to take the children's food and throw it to the dogs" (v. 27). Matthew adds more details to the story. According to him, Jesus does not even care and it was his disciples who urged him to respond, though their suggestion was not too kind either. They said, "Send her away, for she keeps shouting after us" (Matt. 15: 23).

The reasoning behind Jesus's words seems to be clear, even if uncharacteristic of him. He wanted to uphold the primacy and the priority of Israel in his ministry: "Let the children be fed first" (v. 27). Matthew portrays Jesus as even more parochial: "I was sent only to the lost sheep of the house of Israel," says Jesus (Matt. 15: 24). Sounds like Jesus is stating categorically: "*My* people come first!" But that is not all! Jesus also insults the woman by using the epithet 'dogs,' commonly used to describe gentiles. However, the woman, unwilling to back down, responds, or rather retorts, "Even the dogs under the table eat the children's crumbs" (v. 28). Though she is not offensive, and in fact, sounds humble, she does make her point: that no one can be exempt from divine grace, and Jesus cannot ignore and turn a blind eye to her and her daughter's suffering.

Teacher becomes Student

This miracle is rather unusual in that it does not match with other Gospel stories about Jesus, his compassion, and his work among the poor and the marginalised. This is a story which embarrasses Christians, and often we feel compelled, albeit desperately and frustratingly, to defend Jesus's unsympathetic and rather rude response to the Syrophoenician woman. Here we see Jesus, who is usually the wittier one, and good at 'giving back' to those who challenge him, meeting his match. Yet, this is the Gospel, Gospel of our Lord. There is a reason for this text to be placed in the Bible. Therefore, rather than try to defend Jesus or overlook the issues in the text, we have to acknowledge the difficulties and accept it, and learn from it, by turning our attention towards the woman.

We saw that, according to Mark (and Matthew), the woman was a gentile who symbolised all gentiles. This means that she was not only ethnically an outsider, she was also a 'religious other' for Jesus. Though the understanding and practice of religious traditions was different in first century Roman Empire, the multiple emphasis on her non-Jewish identity indicates that she was from a different religious tradition than that of Jesus. It is such a person who tells Jesus to change his opinion and approach, not only towards her, but also, if we recall what she stood for, all gentiles. This gentile religious other, a woman (in a society that was predominantly patriarchal), tells Jesus what he must do. The popular Jewish teacher learns from a person of a different religious tradition. The gentile woman takes Jesus to school. Jesus not only learns to respect the woman and her needs, but also to respect her faith. She opens his mind to go beyond his own ethnic and religious group. No wonder that after this interreligious encounter and learning Jesus appreciates her faith (Matthew 15: 28).

Text in our Context

Christians often look down on other religious traditions as false and invalid. It is often felt that there is nothing much to learn from other religions. But this incident in Jesus's ministry points to the importance of interreligious learning. Though we do not know what religious tradition the woman practised, nevertheless, Jesus appreciates what she had to offer him and his followers. He accepts and acknowledges that he has learnt from this woman.

As the community of believers who follow Jesus Christ, what does this mean for us? Doesn't it mean that we also should be willing to learn from those who are, seemingly, our religious other? If our Lord was willing to be humble, to be corrected, and to change his opinion and his attitude towards others by a person from another religious tradition, his church should also be open to learning from her religious neighbours.

To ponder:

1. *What are the reasons for Jesus going to Tyre and Sidon?*

2. *Mark notes that Jesus did not want to be seen. Why?*

3. *Was Jesus trying to avoid contact with the local people?*

4. *Was Jesus uncomfortable to be in a gentile space?*

5. *Who was Jesus living with? Was his host a gentile, or a Jew who lived in that region?*

6. *What is the name of the woman? Why is her name not mentioned in both the Gospels?*

7. *What could have happened after the healing of her daughter?*

For Discussion

1. *What are some of the difficulties in this interpretation of the text?*

2. *How does it feel to Jesus as a learner and not as a teacher? Is it in line with the tradition of the church?*

Bibliography

Lee, Minkyu. *The Breaking of Bread and the Breaking of Boundaries: A Study of the Metaphor of Bread in the Gospel of Matthew.* New York: Peter Lang, 2015.

Liturgy 1

Freedom and Harmonious living:
A Challenge for a Pluralistic World

Call to Worship

L: With Spirit of Togetherness and mutuality let us worship God who is the source of our existence and freedom.

All: With love and respect for all, let us join to worship God who continues to reveal herself in various and diverse ways.

Opening Prayer

L: God of freedom, we thank you for the gift of life. The universe is your creation, both seen and unseen. Our thoughts and ideas are finite; with each day we discover new things about creation and the human predicament within it. Help us realise that our success in life depends on effective and sustained interdependence with nature and humans.

All: Let shared respect and love for our neighbour be the purpose of our existence. Let not our independence become a hindrance to others. Help us to worship you in truth acknowledging each other's uniqueness. In Jesus's name we pray. Amen.

Invocation

There can be a performance or dance or songs that explicate the importance of togetherness in a pluralistic society.

Adoration

L: Let us adore God who is compassionate and forgiving.

All: We adore you, Lord.

L: Let us adore Jesus Christ, who commanded us to love our neighbours.

All: We adore you, Lord Jesus.

L: Let us adore the never-ending guidance of the Holy Spirit.

All: We adore you, Triune God.

Scripture: Mark 12: 28-34

Sermon: Freedom and Harmonious Living: A Challenge for Pluralistic World

Confession

L: Dear God, we have neither loved you nor our neighbours. Our myopic and limited understandings of religion and fundamental attitudes have hampered the experience of life in its fullness.

All: O God, have mercy on us.

L: God, we have certainly failed to keep your greatest commandment, 'to love your neighbour as yourself.'

All: O God, forgive us and lead us to the freedom of loving others as ourselves.

L: We have failed to serve Christ in this world, we have neglected his mission and the message of God's reign where the oppressed and suffering find preference.

All: Forgive us, O Lord, for we have continued to serve you through mission that is oppressive and divides the world between sinners and non-sinners. We have been inward-looking and selfish.

L: We confess that we have failed to respect people who are not like us. We continue to discriminate them on the basis of caste, colour, creed, gender, sexual orientation and many more things.

All: Forgive us, O Lord, for we have neglected the spirituality of togetherness.

Absolution

L: Forgive us, O Lord.

All: Let us be assured of God's forgiveness if we have honestly confessed our sins. May the Lord transform our attitudes and approaches towards others and instil in us an attitude that seeks to build inclusive communities that are built on shared experiences and peace.

Affirmation

We believe in God who is the source of our lives and also beyond our understanding. We believe in Jesus Christ, who broke all barriers through his inclusive message of God's reign. We believe in the Holy Spirit which empowers us to demolish exclusive approaches and strategies that become source of division. We believe in the holy catholic church which is called to carry out the inclusive mission of Jesus Christ. We believe in the Trinity which teaches us the values of togetherness and interdependence. We believe in the hope that the Resurrection offers us. May it inspire us to put into practice the love shown by Jesus Christ which was unconditional and for all.

Intercession

L: Renew us, O Lord, in the power of your Spirit.

All: Shake us up that we may serve you with commitment and gladness.

L: Lord, we pray for unity and peace in the world.

All: Bring an end to all evil forces that perpetuate violence and fundamentalism which threaten peace within communities, countries and creation.

L: Lord, we pray for the people of our nation.

All: Especially for those who are marginalised and are voiceless. Let their voices be heard and let there be life in its fullness for all.

L: Lord, we pray for your church and its leaders.

All: Give them strength and help them to inspire people who work towards forming a society based on the principle of truth, love and justice.

L: Lord, bless us all.

All: Encourage us, God, to cross all the boundaries that divide us. Help us to promote love, peace and justice and at the same time strive for it. Amen.

The Lord's Prayer

Our God in Heaven…

Benediction

L: Let us depart from here seeking the grace and guidance of God. Let us be committed in serving humanity at large and also to promote humanhood. May the blessing of the triune God be with us, help us and guide us in a life that is characterised by love for all.

All: Amen.

Justice:
Divine Imperative in a Plural World

Call to Worship

Dear God, open our eyes to see you in our midst. Even though human beings adhere to different religions and follow various paths they deem right for their salvation, help us to realise that injustice is a threat to every religion. Let us be challenged by it and not overlook it as just another secular issue. Injustice destroys love, equality, peace and many more virtues that are essential to ideal human life. It exposes oppressions and oppressors. It is a hindrance in the establishment of a community. Open our eyes to the suffering of the world so that we are able to make efforts to transform it and move towards a world that is equal, happy and strong.

Opening Prayer

Dear God, let this time of worship be a liberating experience for all of us. Help us to realise that it is human action that perpetuates injustice. It is not only human beings that suffer, but the created order too suffers because of human actions. Injustice is thus an experience of both humanity and creation.

Draw us close during this worship and help us to realise the dangers of human actions. Help us also to effectively analyse all those who benefit from the unequal order of the world so that those who suffer are not neglected. Liberate us from our own bondages that result from selfishness and docile attitudes in the face of oppression. Amen.

Affirmation of Faith

L: We believe in equality of both humanity and nature. We affirm the integrity of the whole created order. We believe that all those who are neglected, oppressed and marginalised have their own voices that seek liberation from an unjust world. We affirm our partnership with the oppressed in their liberation struggle. We also affirm that justice is integral to every religion. Every religion demands from its followers to be seekers of justice. We also affirm that justice is a religious virtue whereas injustice is a religious threat. Inspire our actions in the present world, O God, so that liberation becomes a lived experience. Amen

Scripture Reading

Bhagavad Gita, Chapter 4: 7-8

"Arjuna, whenever righteousness is on the decline, unrighteousness is in the ascendant, then I am reincarnated. For the protection of the virtuous, for the extirpation of the evil-doers, and for establishing Dharma [righteousness] on a firm footing, I am born from age to age."

Quran 4:135

"Believers! Be upholders of justice, and bearers of witness to truth for the sake of Allah, even though it may either be against yourselves or against your parents and kinsmen, or the rich or the poor: for Allah is more concerned with their well-being than you are. Do not, then, follow your own desires lest you keep away from justice. If you twist or turn away from (the truth), know that Allah is well aware of all that you do."

Luke 4: 18-19

"The Spirit of the Lord is on me, because he has anointed me to proclaim good news to the poor. He has sent me to proclaim freedom for the prisoners and recovery of sight for the blind, to set the oppressed free, to proclaim the year of the Lord's favour."

Sermon: Justice: A Divine Imperative in a Plural World

Confession

We confess that we have been oppressors because we have remained silent in situations of injustice. We have forsaken religious teachings about justice and concentrated on building numbers to prove our superiority over others. We have failed to make justice the centre of our lives. We confess that we are captives of our own comfort zones characterised by ignorance and individualistic motives of salvation. We serve ourselves and have failed to serve others. We have not shown compassion towards the marginalised. We recognise our shortcomings in the face of discrimination.

Absolution

Let us be assured that God forgives us. Let us be united in fighting injustice and that in our fight forgiveness will be out into practice.

Intercession

L: Dear God, you love all equally, you alone are holy. We pray for those who face structural violence and discrimination and are undergoing pain due to such discriminative tendencies, those who are on the receiving end on the basis of caste, race, creed, class, gender, colour, sexual orientation, and so on. Help us to break life-negating realities and all that is the source of dehumanisation. Lord, in your Mercy...

All: Hear our Prayer

L: We pray for those who are suffering from poverty and unequal distribution of wealth. We remember the present economic system that perpetuates poverty. We seek your guidance in our resistance to such oppressive systems that create inequality. Lord, in your Mercy...

All: Hear our Prayer

L: Help us to rise above religious barriers that create divisions. Let us therefore pray for religious unity and harmony in the world. Help us to realise that the movement of the Spirit is not bound by a particular religion or doctrines. Help us to live in religious harmony and in recognising the fact that God works in various and diverse ways, through various and diverse intuitions which are beyond our understanding, for the establishment of a just world. Help us, O God, to unite in making this world a better place for all to live in. Lord, in your Mercy...

All: Hear our prayer.

Prayer of Commitment

All: We wish to dedicate ourselves for the cause of justice.

We value the integrity of human beings and creation.

We affirm that equality is the best virtue to live by.

We recognise that our life is threatened by discrimination

Give us the courage to transform discriminative attitudes and actions

We express our solidarity with all those who suffer.

We endeavour to create loving and sharing communities.

We seek to build a society that enjoys its differences.

We endeavour to move towards a world which is built on peace and love.

Benediction

Let us go into this world to rebuild that which is broken and to heal that which is wounded. Let God empower us to be leaders that seek to establish justice. Let our communion inspire us to work together in promoting life-affirming values. Let justice and peace be experienced by all. May the blessings of God, who is beyond our understanding, be with us all in our efforts that seek liberation.

All: **Hear our Prayer**

Afterword

Peniel Jesudason Rufus Rajkumar*

The Namibian missiologist Lamin Sanneh once wrote, "For all of us pluralism can be a rock of stumbling, but for God it is the cornerstone of the universal design".[1] The difficulty of aligning religious diversity alongside God's purposes for the world has been a part of the experience of many South Asian Christians. Growing up as a Christian in India, I often realised that despite being deeply immersed in the reality of religious diversity, opportunities to reflect on the implications of this reality within a church context were limited. The only light at the end of this 'theological tunnel' that many churches could offer was the biblical idea of being 'a light to the nations'. This reinforced a 'missional' pattern of relating 'to' (I am deliberately avoiding the word 'with' here) our neighbours of other faiths.

However, there have been changes in Christian attitudes to other faiths over time. In the Asian context where Christianity is a 'small watering hole' amidst the 'sea of religions' there has been an increase in openness to other religious experiences and traditions. This interreligious sensibility has meant that "the abundance within God is reclaimed graciously and generously in order to re-member and re-integrate local and native cultural and religious experiences and traditions, and thus to reclaim the identity of Asian communities that were fragmented and overpowered by colonial forms of Christianity".[2] This reclamation process primarily assumed the form of inculturation and interreligious dialogue. Nonetheless, these processes too haven't been without their problems.

Often such forms of engagement with religious diversity have been unapologetically elitist in their orientation and thereby estranged from and irrelevant to the margins—"the deliberately silenced, or the preferably unheard,"[3] who are undermined by and sidelined from the ubiquitous centres of power. The conceptual womb from which Christian engagement with religious diversity was born maintained an umbilical severance from the experiences and perspectives of the margins that the resultant brain child was completely estranged from the margins. It is this anomaly that the present volume addresses with courage and conviction.

In many ways this volume is not just a timely intervention but also a necessary irruption of the ways in which Christian theologians and churches have engaged with the question of religious diversity. By embracing the perspective of the margins, which have 'a disturbing revelatory potential, the potential of disclosure and the power of exposure'[4] this books opens readers to provocative and prophetic ways of engaging with religious diversity.

All this makes sense in the global context which many have described using the imperial language of the empire. The empire in its various manifestations has ensured that "the assault on vulnerable, fragile, sections of society is at once so complete, so cruel, and so clever—all encompassing and yet specifically targeted, blatantly brutal and yet unbelievably insidious — that its sheer audacity has eroded our definition of justice".[5] Therefore, it is all the more important to eschew any methodology which derives tacit support from the centres of power. As we have been warned, in the context of empire, there is always a danger that 'we will continue to support empire by default unless we look for those particular and often repressed places where we encounter alternatives'.[6] Therefore, there is always need for us to look for and learn from 'below the surface of the powers that be' and 'between the lines of the status quo'.[7] By embracing a methodology that is 'upside down' the authors redeem and reclaim interreligious engagement as a tool that can be employed in the pursuit of justice, peace and the integrity of creation.

This volume is part of a daring series of publications that has taken up the challenge of 'Reimagining Church as Event' from the perspectives of the margins. In a global political context where politicians have usurped the 'politics of spectacle' — this series is an important intervention to redeem the theological significance of 'event' from hollow optics and empty rhetoric. For Christians any understanding of the 'event-ness' of the Church stems from the 'Christ event' — the embodied enactment of God's liberative love unfolded in the 'events' of the incarnation, cross and resurrection. To reimage itself as event in the context of religious diversity the church needs to 'counter-actualize' Christ's love in the midst of practices of vilification, violation and violence. This inevitably entails solidarity with the margins because the 'Christ-event' by itself is a narrative of solidarity with the margins. It is the story of the marginal one who in his incarnation comes to his own and is rejected by them (cf. John 1:11); who in his crucifixion suffers 'outside the city gates' (Hebrew 13:12) and who in his resurrection while proclaiming victory over suffering and death yet bears the scars of the cross.

The language of church as event has the capacity to address churches in the language of the indicative, the imperative and the interrogative — probing us to explore who we are and what we ought to do.[8] As a volume which invites readers to rethink traditional ways of being Church in the face of religious diversity, this publication is also a call to the churches to not just be spectators of the gospel but rather become, what the Brazilian theatre activist Augusto Boal calls, 'spec-actors' — people who do not watch a play as spectators but participate in the narrative infusing it with new meanings and possibilities. From a Christian perspective, the one question it raises for churches is: How can we as churches insert ourselves into God's unfolding script of universal goodness and grace as an interruptive and interpretive presence — courageously interrupting injustice in all forms and compassionately interpreting the gospel through good deeds? In answering these questions will churches rediscover what it means to reimagine themselves as event in a multireligious world.

Endnotes

* **The Rev. Dr. Peniel Jesudason Rufus Rajkumar** serves the World Council of Churches as Programme Coordinator, Interreligious Dialogue and Cooperation.

[1] Lamin Sanneh, *Translating the Message: The Missionary Impact on Culture*, (Maryknoll, NY: Orbis, 1989), p.27.

[2] Sathianathan Clarke, *'The Task, Method and Content of Asian Theologies'*, in Peniel Jesudason Rufus Rajkumar, ed *Asian Theology on the Way: Christianity, Culture and Context*, (London: SPCK, 2012), (pp.3-13), p.8.

[3] Arundhati Roy, 'Peace and the New Corporate Liberation Theology', in *An Ordinary Person's Guide to the Empire*, (New Delhi: Penguin Books, 2005), p.242.

[4] Vitor Westhelle, 'Margins Exposed: Representation, Hybridity and Transfiguration', in R.S. Sugirtharajah (ed.), *Still At the Margins: Biblical Scholarship Fifteen Years After Voices From the Margins*, (London: T & T Clark, 2008), (pp.68-87), p.69.

[5] Arundhati Roy, 'Peace and the New Corporate Liberation Theology", p.242.

[6] Jeorg Reiger, *Christ and Empire: From Paul to Postcolonial Times,* (Augsburg: Fortress, 2007), p.315.

[7] Reiger, *Christ and Empire,* p.317.

[8] David F. Ford, *Christian Wisdom: Desiring God and Learning in Love,* (Cambridge: Cambridge University Press, 2007), pp.4ff.